PEARL JAM
TRIVIA BOOK

Uncover The Epic History & Facts
Every Fan Should Know!

By

Dale Raynes

Bridge Press
dp@purplelink.org

Please consider writing a review!
Just visit: purplelink.org/review

ISBN: 978-1-955149-08-2

TABLE OF CONTENTS

INTRODUCTION

Pearl Jam was the most popular rock band in the world in the early 1990s. When grunge ruled the airwaves of MTV and the festival circuit, they outsold all their peers. They have also proved to be the longest-lasting of all their major peers. As other bands fell prey to deaths and internal disputes, Pearl Jam has stuck it out. And aside from switching a drummer here and there, they have maintained the same core of gifted musicians. That is why Pearl Jam is a well-oiled machine of a band.

Aside from the high quality of their music over the years, Pearl Jam's most notable characteristic is its integrity. It has never sold out and never attempted to ride with prevailing fashion. At first, they were criticized for being too mainstream in an era where being punk and alternative was considered cool. Later they were considered an antiquated group of unfashionable dinosaurs. Other bands wilted under the pressure of expectations, but not Pearl Jam. They just went on doing their thing, which just happened to be creating first-rate hard rock.

While most would consider their debut album *Ten* to be the band's finest offering, a review of their

1

discography reveals incredible depth and consistency. Ask hardcore fans what their favorite album is, and you will get a wide and varied array of answers spanning several decades.

Aside from their high-quality recordings, perhaps the most remarkable element of the Pearl Jam mystique arises from their live shows. If you have been to one of their concerts—and I have been to more than my fair share—you will never forget it. They never play the same set-list. It always goes on for at least three hours, and the energy never ebbs for a second. Also, Eddie never misses a note. There is a reason their shows are so widely bootlegged. Pearl Jam is easily the best live band of their generation and one of the best of all time.

Think you are a true fan? Do you know everything there is to know about this fantastic Seattle band? Let's find out in this Pearl Jam trivia extravaganza.

CHAPTER 1:

CHILDHOOD AND EARLY DAYS

1. Which of these rock legends DOESN'T share a birthday with Andrew Wood?

    a. Elvis Presley
    b. Robbie Krieger
    c. Jim Morrison
    d. David Bowie

2. When did Andrew Wood start smoking weed?

    a. Age ten
    b. Age twelve
    c. Age sixteen
    d. Age twenty

3. When asked what genre of music he sang, what did Andrew famously reply?

    a. Love rock
    b. Hard glam
    c. Flash grunge
    d. Funky monkey

4. What last name was Eddie Vedder born with?

    a. Vedder
    b. Severson
    c. Mueller
    d. Louis

5. Eddie had trouble in adolescence and dropped out of high school. Which high school was it?

    a. San Dieguito High School Academy
    b. Torrey Pines High School
    c. Canyon Crest Academy
    d. La Costa Canyon High School

6. What first name was Stone Gossard born with?

    a. Carpenter
    b. Gregory
    c. Franklin
    d. Stone

7. In which state did Jeff Ament grow up?

    a. Washington
    b. Oregon
    c. Montana
    d. Idaho

8. Why did Jeff quit college?

    a. To pursue a music career
    b. He was a bad student
    c. To pay his bills
    d. They discontinued his program

9. Where did drummer Dave Krusen grow up?

    a. Gig Harbor
    b. Tacoma
    c. Spokane
    d. Bellevue

10. When Eddie wrote his first lyrics, he was under the influence of what?

    a. Prescribed medication
    b. Alcohol
    c. Marijuana
    d. Lack of sleep

11. The song Jeremy refers to with a kid shooting up his classroom. Was it based on a true experience Eddie had?

    a. Yes
    b. Sort of
    c. No
    d. A close friend of his experienced it

12. Where did current drummer Matt Cameron grow up?

    a. Seattle, WA
    b. San Diego, CA
    c. Portland, OR
    d. Reno, NV

13. Matt Cameron's first band was a cover band. The band they were paying tribute to sued them for copy infringement. What band was it?

a. Led Zeppelin
b. Rush
c. The Rolling Stones
d. Kiss

14. In 1978, Matt contributed a song to a movie under the pseudonym Foo Cameron. What movie was it?

    a. *Attack of the Killer Tomatoes*
    b. *Game of Death*
    c. *Piranha*
    d. *Puff the Magic Dragon*

15. When Matt first arrived in Seattle, how did he pay the rent?

    a. He worked as a barista at Starbucks
    b. He pumped gas
    c. He made enough from drumming
    d. He flipped copies at Kinko's

16. At what age did Mike start to play the guitar?

    a. Seven
    b. Nine
    c. Eleven
    d. Fifteen

17. Mike's band Shadow moved to L.A. in 1986. How did things go for them?

    a. They played some shows but couldn't get a break
    b. They released an E.P. but couldn't get a record deal

c. They broke up on the first day in L.A.

d. They couldn't get a show down there

18. Which future member of Red Hot Chili Peppers was in the high school band Chain Reaction with Jack Irons?

a. Flea

b. Anthony Kiedis

c. Hillel Slovak

d. Jack Sherman

19. Before briefly joining Pearl Jam, Matt Chamberlain played for what one-hit-wonder late 80s and early 90s band?

a. Edie Brickell & New Bohemians

b. Blind Melon

c. Sherriff

d. L.A. Guns

20. In which state did drummer Dave Abbruzzese grow up?

a. Washington

b. Texas

c. Connecticut

d. California

ANSWERS

1. C- Jim Morrison

2. B- Age twelve

3. Love rock

4. Severson

5. San Dieguito High School Academy

6. Stone

7. Montana

8. They discontinued his program. Jeff was in the graphic design program at the University of Montana.

9. Gig Harbor

10. D- Lack of sleep: he was working the night shift at hotels and gas stations.

11. Sort of. When he was in junior high, a fellow student shot up a fish tank.

12. San Diego, CA

13. Kiss: Matt was surprised when he met Paul Stanley, and he did not seem to have a problem.

14. *Attack of the Killer Tomatoes*

15. He flipped copies at Kinko's.

16. Eleven: before that, he often played the bongos.

17. They couldn't get a show down there.

18. Hillel Slovak

19. Edie Brickell & New Bohemians

20. Texas

DID YOU KNOW?

- Andrew Wood used the stage name Landrew the Love Child when he performed with his first bands. He usually dressed in drag, sometimes in very skimpy lingerie when he did so. Andrew — sorry, Landrew the Love Child — also wore thick white face paint and jokingly picked fights with the audience members.

- Eddie's biological father was Edward Louis Severson. However, his mother and father separated when he was very small, and his mother remarried Peter Mueller. For years Eddie believed Mueller was his biological father, and his three stepbrothers were his biological siblings. When Eddie discovered the truth, it destabilized his life considerably. By that time, his biological father had passed away from multiple sclerosis. The experience was the inspiration for "Alive", one of Pearl Jam's best-known songs.

- Mike was inspired to play guitar by 80s blues genius Stevie Ray Vaughn. McCready had played guitar for a while but gave it up. However, he attended a Stevie Ray Vaughn and Double Trouble show at the Gorge Amphitheater in the city of George, Washington (yes, that is what it is called.) As Mike remembers: "As soon as he started

"Couldn't Stand the Weather," these huge clouds rolled in overhead, and rain started pouring down. When the song ended, the rain stopped! It was like a religious experience, and it changed me. It lifted me out of the negative mindset I was in, and it got me playing again. I thank him forever for that."

- Jack Irons would later play for Pearl Jam, but he also played a crucial role in establishing the band. Stone and Jeff asked Jack if he wanted to join their new band, and he turned them down. However, he passed the band's demo to Eddie Vedder, who contacted the band as a result.

CHAPTER 2:

MAKING THE JAM: THE PRE-PEARL JAM BANDS

1. In what year was Pearl Jam's precursor band, Green River, formed?

    a. 1983
    b. 1984
    c. 1985
    d. 1986

2. Why did the band call itself Green River?

    a. After the Creedence Clearwater Revival song
    b. After a river near Jeff Ament's home
    c. After a serial killer
    d. It just sounded cool

3. Which alternative band quoted a Green River song in one of their releases?

    a. Sonic Youth
    b. The Melvins
    c. Bad Religion
    d. My Bloody Valentine

4. Which label released Green River's first E.P. *Come on Down*?

    a. Reciprocal Recording
    b. Sub Pop
    c. Homestead Records
    d. C/Z Records

5. Mark Arm clashed with Jeff Ament and Stone Gossard when they were in Green River together. What did he accuse them of?

    a. Being bad musicians
    b. Taking too many drugs
    c. Being too mainstream
    d. Not being mainstream enough

6. Which band did Mark Arm form after Green River?

    a. The Screaming Trees
    b. Mudhoney
    c. The U-Men
    d. The Melvins

7. Where was charismatic Mother Love Bone frontman, Andrew Wood, born?

    a. Seattle, Washington
    b. Columbus, Mississippi
    c. Morgantown, West Virginia
    d. Athens, Georgia

8. Before becoming the lead singer of Mother Love Bone, Andrew Wood was the lead singer of what band?

    a. Malfunkshun
    b. The U-Men
    c. Skin Yard
    d. Love Battery

9. Before changing their name to Mother Love Bone, what was the first name of the band Wood, Ament, and Gossard formed?

    a. Temple of the Dog
    b. Lords of the Wasteland
    c. Tad
    d. The Walkabouts

10. When Mother Love Bone was first courted by L.A. music executives, what attracted their attention to the Seattle scene?

    a. The breakthrough of Nirvana
    b. Starbucks coffee
    c. The popularity of Soundgarden
    d. Duff McKagan came from there

11. Which record company ended up signing Mother Love Bone?

    a. Sub Pop
    b. Columbia
    c. Polygram
    d. Geffen

12. Which 80s rock mainstay did Mother Love Bone open for?

    a. Ratt
    b. The Dogs D'Amour
    c. L.A. Guns
    d. W.A.S.P.

13. Where did Mother Love Bone record its stunning debut album *Apple*?

    a. Seattle
    b. Sausalito
    c. L.A.
    d. San Diego

14. Which classic by another Seattle band was written about Andrew Wood?

    a. "Would?" by Alice in Chains
    b. "Blackhole Sun" by Soundgarden
    c. "Lithium" by Nirvana
    d. "Nearly Lost You" by the Screaming Trees

15. In what year did the members of Mother Love Bone reunite, with singer Shawn Smith on vocals?

    a. 1997
    b. 2003
    c. 2005
    d. 2010

16. What was the first band where Mike McCready cooperated with Stone Gossard and Jeff Ament?

a. Green River
b. Mother Love Bone
c. Temple of the Dog
d. Pearl Jam

17. In San Diego, Eddie played in a band called Indian Style. Which well-known drummer was also part of that band?

    a. Chad Smith, later of the Red Hot Chili Peppers
    b. Stephen Perkins, later of Jane's Addiction
    c. Travis Barker, later of Blink 182
    d. Brad Wilk, later of Rage Against the Machine

18. In what year did Temple of the Dog launch a short reunion tour?

    a. 1998
    b. 2007
    c. 2012
    d. 2016

19. Who was the drummer on the Temple of the Dog album?

    a. Matt Cameron
    b. Greg Gilmore
    c. Dave Abbruzzese
    d. Jack Irons

20. When did Pearl Jam first play Andrew Wood's signature song "Crown of Thorns" live?

    a. 1994

b. 1998
c. 2000
d. 2018

ANSWERS

1. B-1984

2. After a serial killer. The Green River Killer was found guilty of committing forty-nine murders in 2001. At the time Green River played, the identity of the killer was unknown. We won't mention his name because we celebrate grunge heroes and not murderers.

3. Sonic Youth. Green River opened for Sonic Youth when they played in Seattle. Sonic Youth then quoted the song "Come on Down" in their song "Nevermind (What Was It Anyway)".

4. Homestead Records: Sub Pop rejected Green River for not being grunge enough! However, they signed the band later.

5. Being too mainstream: the future Pearl Jam members wanted a significant recording contract, and Arm wished to pursue a more punk rock sound.

6. Mudhoney

7. Columbus, Mississippi

8. Malfunkshen

9. Lords of the Wasteland

10. Duff McKagan came from there. This was the height of the popularity of Guns N' Roses.

11. Polygram

12. B- The Dogs D'Amour

13. B- Sausalito: they recorded it at the Record Plant branch in that California city.

14. "Would?" by Alice in Chains

15. 2010

16. Temple of the Dog

17. Brad Wilk, later of Rage Against the Machine

18. 2016

19. Matt Cameron

20. 2000

DID YOU KNOW?

- Andrew Wood tragically overdosed on heroin in March 1990, just days before Mother Love Bone's debut album *Apple* was due release. Andrew had just given an interview where he expressed his excitement at the forthcoming album: "I want the world to know that Mother Love Bone is coming to take over the world, a plethora of delights, a fruit salad compote of delights." The singer had been clean for a while but seemed to have relapsed that night and was discovered in bad condition by his girlfriend. He was kept alive for a couple of days to allow friends and family to say goodbye. Wood was cremated, and his ashes were laid to rest at Miller-Woodlawn Memorial Park in Bremerton, Washington.

- The album *Apple* was highly critically acclaimed upon its release and remains in high regard today. It most notably received a rave review from *Rolling Stone* magazine. The review compared the band favorably to Led Zeppelin. *The New York Times*, not usually a promoter of hard rock excellence, noted that "*Apple* may be one of the first great hard-rock records of the 90s," and that "Andrew Wood could have been the first of the big-league Seattle rock stars." We couldn't agree more.

- Legendary Soundgarden singer Chris Cornell was Andrew Wood's roommate. At the time, Andrew's girlfriend, Xana La Fuente, joked that Andy and Chris would have fallen in love if one of them were a girl. Though the two amazing singers wrote a few songs together, they did not survive aside from the music of Island of Summer. Cornell's idea was to put together Temple of the Dog, a tribute project to honor the deceased singer.

- Andrew Wood's girlfriend, Xana La Fuente, did not believe Cornell's tribute to the Mother Love Bone singer was sincere. She posted that the Temple of the Dog reunion tour was nothing but a "cash grab" on the Soundgarden singer's part. La Fuente accused Cornell of denying her partial lyric writing credits to the song "Times of Trouble" and stealing all of Andrew's possessions from her.

- Jack Irons was one of Red Hot Chili Peppers' founding members, joining his childhood friend Hillel Slovak. When Slovak died of a heroin overdose in 1988, both bassist Flea and singer Anthony Kiedis did not attend the funeral, considering the situation to be "too surreal." Irons sank into a depression and decided to quit the band. He said he did not want to be part of a band that was killing his friends. In 2006, Irons said, "What happened to Hillel still haunts me today. I was devastated, torn apart, and wrecked emotionally. I'm still suffering from depression and still being treated for it. It was like my world was shattered too when he died, and the dreams we dreamed died with him. But I'm overjoyed by the band's success today. What they've achieved is a massive tribute to Hillel. Had he lived, he would undoubtedly have become one of rock's legendary guitarists."

CHAPTER 3:

FORMING PEARL JAM

1. Which childhood toy did Mike McCready carry around and take pictures of band members and friends with?

    a. A teddy bear
    b. A Cabbage Patch doll
    c. A Curious George doll
    d. A Mr. Potato Head

2. "Alive" had initially been a Mother Love Bone song, performed once in concert. What was that song called?

    a. "Zanzibar"
    b. "Lubricated Muscle Drive"
    c. "Dollar Short"
    d. "Jumpin Jehova"

3. Eddie recorded the vocals to three songs on Jeff and Stone's demo tape as a way of auditioning for Pearl Jam. Which song was NOT on that tape?

    a. "Alive"
    b. "Once"

c. "State of Love and Trust"

d. "Footsteps"

4. Why did Jeff and Stone get drummer Matt Cameron to play on their first demo, even though he wasn't a member of the band?

   a. They considered Matt the best drummer in town

   b. He was a friend, and they didn't feel like auditioning anyone

   c. They were desperate

   d. Matt was auditioning for the band

5. Where did what became Pearl Jam write the songs that would appear on the famous demo they handed off to Jack Irons?

   a. A local studio

   b. A local bar

   c. Stone's parents' attic

   d. Mother Love Bone's rehearsal space

6. Who produced that first demo?

   a. Chris Hanzsek

   b. Jack Endino

   c. Mark Arm

   d. Butch Vig

7. Jack and Eddie met at a gig. Who was playing?

   a. The Red Hot Chili Peppers

   b. Joe Strummer

   c. The Pixies

    d. Creedle

8. Where was Eddie when he first heard the demo that Stone and Jeff had recorded?

    a. His L.A. apartment
    b. On the beach in San Diego
    c. A Chevron warehouse
    d. In Seattle

9. The demo had a song called "Agyptian Crave". After Eddie wrote the lyrics to it, what would the song eventually be called?

    a. "Dirty Frank"
    b. "Brother"
    c. "Once"
    d. "Porch"

10. Eddie recorded the demo tape over a compilation cassette. Which artist did it feature?

    a. Merle Haggard
    b. The Clash
    c. Johnny Cash
    d. The Who

11. How soon after Stone and Jeff had heard the demo tape did Eddie find out that he got the job?

    a. The same day
    b. A week later
    c. Two weeks later
    d. A month later

12. Eddie turned the instrumental track "E Ballad" into "Black" after writing the moving lyrics. When did he write them?

    a. Before he recorded his demo
    b. Right after sending the demo
    c. After he got the job but before arriving in Seattle
    d. After arriving in Seattle

13. One day before leaving for Seattle to join up with the band, Eddie saw Soundgarden in California. What was the name of the festival they were playing?

    a. A Gathering of the Tribes
    b. Ohana Festival
    c. Beyond Wonderland
    d. Aftershock

14. When the band first came together, they were named Mookie Blaylock, after one of the band's favorite basketball players. What team did Mookie play for at the time?

    a. Seattle Supersonics
    b. L.A. Lakers
    c. New Jersey Nets
    d. Golden State Warriors

15. In 1991, the band played a few dates on the West Coast in what is remembered as the "Mookie Blaylock Tour." Who were they supporting in most of those shows?

    a. Soundgarden

b. Alice in Chains
c. Mudhoney
d. The Misfits

16. Mookie Blaylock played the legendary Marquee club on their first tour. In what capacity did they play?

a. They headlined the show
b. They were part of a bill of several bands
c. They opened for Mudhoney
d. They opened for Green Jelly

17. Where did the band announce that they had changed their name to Pearl Jam?

a. During a show in L.A.
b. On a Seattle radio show
c. In a press release
d. In posters advertising their first show as Pearl Jam

18. True or False: Eddie also crafted artwork for the demo tape he recorded to audition. It included his face, prison bars, and sperm fertilizing an egg.

19. True or False: Eddie had never met Stone or Jeff before being offered the job as lead singer.

20. True or False: Eddie's duet with Chris Cornell on the song Hunger Strike was the first time his voice appeared on a record.

ANSWERS

1. A Mr. Potato Head. There is a fairly hilarious picture of Chris Cornell with the toy on his head.

2. "Dollar Short"

3. "Footsteps"

4. They considered Matt the best drummer in town.

5. Stone's parents' attic

6. Chris Hanzsek

7. Joe Strummer: Eddie was a roadie for the former Clash singer, and Jack was playing in his band.

8. A Chevron warehouse. He was working the graveyard shift there at the time.

9. "Once"

10. Merle Haggard

11. A week later. However, they decided that he was hired the day they heard him. The problem was that they could not get ahold of him.

12. After he got the job but before arriving in Seattle.

13. New Jersey Nets: he was a damn good player too. Mookie was an all-star in 1994 and averaged 13.5 points per game over his long career. Unfortunately,

his post-basketball life has not gone as well. He was charged with vehicular homicide for his part in a DUI accident and was incarcerated for three years.

14. A Gathering of the Tribes: it was a one-time festival in Irvine, organized by Ian Astbury of the Cult and legendary promoter Bill Graham.

15. Alice in Chains: the Seattle band was starting to blow up on the strength of their outstanding Facelift debut album.

16. They opened for Green Jelly. I can only imagine how well the earnest songs about Eddie's childhood went with Green Jelly's weird songs like Whip Me Teenage Babe and Eat Satan's Ham.

17. On a Seattle radio show. The station was KISW, in case you are keeping score.

18. True: Eddie also wrote the date in White Out. It was September 13, 1990.

19. False: this is an often-repeated myth. Jack made introductions between them in L.A. previously. Eddie met the other guys at least once before recording the demo, and possibly up to three times. Stone told Seattle radio's KXRX, "We met [Eddie] in L.A. and then flew him up two weeks later."

20. True.

DID YOU KNOW?

- When the band that would become Pearl Jam recorded its first singer-less demos, they didn't have a name yet. The producer booked them as "Stone and Co.," which reflected Gossard's role as the driving force behind the band at that time. Though he cannot read music, Gossard set up charts that marked the different music transitions and masterminded the arrangements of all twelve instrumental songs they recorded.

- Mother Love Bone's *Apple* and the publicized death of Andrew Wood created a bit of a buzz around the new band Jeff and Stone were putting together. On a visit to L.A., they talked to the *Los Angeles Times* and *Rolling Stone*. They mentioned that they were looking for a new singer, but Jeff said they hoped for a completely different type of singer from Andy. He explained that "To go out and find another singer who looked like Andy and maybe sang a little bit like Andy would just be prostitution."

- Jack and Eddie played basketball together regularly in L.A., usually on Friday nights. As Jeff recalled later, "Jack had just been hanging out with Eddie, and Ed had been coming up from San Diego and hanging out with [his girlfriend] Beth, who worked in L.A. at the time. Jack and Ed were playing basketball one day, and Jack said, 'Hey man, I got this tape by these guys...'"

- After Eddie first heard the demo tape, he immediately went out surfing. As he surfed, lyrics and images from his childhood surfaced, and the first lyrics of what would become Pearl Jam songs occurred to him. Vedder immediately headed to his girlfriend's house because it was closer than his own home. Eddie wanted to get the lyrics on paper while they were still fresh.

- He wrote the lyrics to "Alive" very quickly. Vedder would later remember: "A situation I felt I could draw from... this strange twist in my life having to do with a father that I didn't know was my father until later in my adolescent years. And then, looking back and realizing the whole time that I was growing up, I was maybe meeting him briefly. I would catch looks on my mom's face once in a while. I don't know what it was, really, but I think she saw my real dad in me. He had been long passed [away]. Sometimes we're a little bit like carbon copies, you know." The song also refers to incest, which Eddie clarifies never happened in real life.

- The song "Once" was also written from the demo tape and was a sequel of sorts to "Alive." Eddie explained that the kid from "Alive" had grown up to become "a serial killer [who'd] been abused by his folks," thus provoking the "nasty things [he did] to other people. That was him going to trial for his crimes or whatever... I had the silly call and answer [verses]. There's like a trial and a jury." Meanwhile, in the song "Footsteps," the same individual was in his jail cell. If so, the first three songs Eddie wrote were essentially a mini-opera in the vein of his musical heroes, the Who.

CHAPTER 4:

A MASTERPIECE OF A DEBUT ALBUM

1. In which Seattle studio did the band record *Ten*?

    a. Orbit Audio Recordings
    b. Evolution Studios
    c. Robert Lang Studios
    d. London Bridge

2. Which song on *Ten* did Pearl Jam refuse to release as a single, despite pressure from Epic Records?

    a. "Even Flow"
    b. "Porch"
    c. "State of Love and Trust"
    d. "Black"

3. "Even Flow" is one of the best-loved songs on the album. How many takes did the band do before they nailed it?

    a. One magical take
    b. Under ten

c. Over twenty

d. Over fifty

4. The song "Footsteps" was recorded and considered for inclusion in the album. What ended up happening to it?

   a. It was rearranged as a song on *Temple of the Dog*

   b. It was released as the B-side to "Jeremy"

   c. It appeared on the *Lost Dogs* compilation

   d. All of the above

5. There are a bunch of unconventional effects used in the song "Oceans." Which of these was used thirty seconds into the track?

   a. A salt shaker and lawnmower

   b. A pepper shaker and fire extinguisher

   c. An olive oil can and vacuum cleaner

   d. A jar of mayonnaise and a garbage disposal unit

6. The song "Yellow Ledbetter" was recorded during the sessions for *Ten* but was not released at the time. When it was eventually released in the compilation *Lost Dogs*, which version did they use?

   a. A live version

   b. The first take

   c. The second take

   d. A later re-recording

7. The song "Jeremy" was not coming together in the sessions. What saved it from being dropped from the album?

    a. Eddie changed the lyrics
    b. The addition of wah-wah guitars
    c. The use of a cello
    d. The addition of a Hammond organ part

8. Why did the band fire Dave Krusen at the end of the sessions for *Ten*?

    a. His drumming was bad
    b. His drinking was out of control
    c. They wanted to temp Matt Cameron into the band
    d. They didn't get along with him

9. Who designed the cover of the album?

    a. Jeff Ament
    b. Stone Gossard
    c. Mike McCready
    d. Eddie Vedder

10. The album producer, Rick Parashar, did not have much experience producing albums before he worked on *Ten*. Aside from *Temple of the Dog*, what was his only previous album as a head producer?

    a. Forced Entry – *Uncertain Future*
    b. Alice in Chains – *Facelift*
    c. Metal Church – *Human Factor*
    d. Sanctuary – *Into the Mirror Black*

11. Which song from the album was significantly stretched out live so that Eddie could climb the scaffolding and do other dangerous things?

  a. "Alive"
  b. "Porch"
  c. "Once"
  d. "Why Go"

12. How many copies did *Ten* sell in the first week after its release?

  a. 25,000
  b. 50,000
  c. 100,000
  d. 200,000

13. Which song from *Ten* has been played live the most?

  a. "Alive"
  b. "Jeremy"
  c. "Even Flow"
  d. "Black"

14. The band has repeatedly expressed dissatisfaction with how the album was produced. What is the main problem with how *Ten* sounds, in their view?

  a. Too much distortion
  b. The vocals are too loud
  c. Too much reverb
  d. The bass is too low in the mix

15. When the band released *Ten* with a new mix and production job, who oversaw the remix?

    a. Jeff Ament
    b. Brendan O'Brien
    c. Don Was
    d. Josh Evans

16. True or False: "State of Love and Trust" was recorded in the *Ten* sessions and then released on the soundtrack for the movie *Singles*.

17. True or False: Jeff wanted the song "Brother" (later released in the *Lost Dogs* compilation) to be included in the album, and Stone felt strongly that it should be cut.

18. True or False: Pearl Jam canceled part of their own tour to promote *Ten* to support the Red Hot Chili Peppers on their Blood Sex Sugar Magik tour.

19. True or False: Pearl Jam played on the same bill as Nirvana for a few shows after the release of *Ten*.

20. True or False: When *Ten* was reissued, it was made available on the *Rock Star* computer game.

ANSWERS

1. London Bridge: Mother Love Bone, Temple of the Dog, and Alice in Chains also recorded there. So did Nickelback for some reason.

2. "Black": the song was too personal for Vedder. "Some songs just aren't meant to be played between hit No. 2 and hit No. 3," The singer told *Rolling Stone* in 1993. "You start doing those things, you'll crush it. That's not why we wrote songs. We didn't write to make hits."

3. Over fifty: Mike later recalled, "I swear to God it was a nightmare. We played that thing over and over until we hated each other."

4. All of the above: the Temple of the Dog song "Times of Trouble" is an adaptation of "Footsteps."

5. B- A pepper shaker and fire extinguisher

6. The second take

7. The use of a cello: as Jeff remembered, "On 'Jeremy,' I always heard this other melody in the choruses and the end, and it never sounded good on guitar or bass. So, we brought in a cello player which inspired a background vocal, and those things made the song really happen. Most of the time, if something doesn't work right away, I just say fuck

it—but this was an instance when perseverance paid off."

8. B- His drinking was out of control. Dave admits that it was his fault. "They had to let me go. I couldn't stop drinking, and it was causing problems. They gave me many chances, but I couldn't get it together."

9. Jeff Ament: if you fold out the entire cover, you can see the band posing in front of a cutout of the words Pearl Jam made by Jeff. The concept was "about really being together as a group and entering into the world of music as a true band... a sort of all-for-one deal."

10. Forced Entry - *Uncertain Future*: a thrash metal album of all things.

11. "Porch"

12. 25,000: it didn't look like the album was going anywhere at first.

13. "Even Flow"

14. Too much reverb

15. Brendan O'Brien: Brendan was hesitant to make a new version of such a beloved classic and turned the band down at first. He said, "The band loved the original mix of *Ten*, but were also interested in what it would sound like if I were to deconstruct and remix it...The original *Ten* sound is what

millions of people bought, dug, and loved, so I was initially hesitant to mess around with that. After years of persistent nudging from the band, I was able to wrap my head around the idea of offering it as a companion piece to the original — giving a fresh take on it, a more direct sound."

16. False: the song "State of Love and Trust" was indeed recorded in the *Ten* sessions. However, a different later version was released on the soundtrack. Ament says that the original version is far better. It was released in the *Rearviewmirror: Greatest Hits* compilation.

17. True: Jeff was so hurt and offended by the decision that he almost quit the band.

18. True: the Chili Peppers were easily the bigger band, and they felt that Jack Irons was doing them a favor by getting them a spot as the support group.

19. True: both played as support for the Red Hot Chili Peppers. Funnily enough, Nirvana was hired to replace Pearl Jam, who were not considered popular enough for the spot. But when the Smashing Pumpkins quit the tour, Pearl Jam kept their place.

20. True.

DID YOU KNOW?

- The band did not particularly believe in the first album. They thought they had good material but had yet to gel as a band fully. Jeff told *Bass Player Magazine*, "We knew we were still a long way from being a real band at that point, and we needed to tour. So essentially, *Ten* was just an excuse to tour. We told the record company, 'We know we can be a great band, so let's just get the opportunity to get out and play.' When it was released, I figured if we sold 100,000 copies, it would be a total success." It sold a bit more than that, Jeff.

- The solo for "Alive" is one of the greatest guitar solos of the '90s. No, really. Just listen to it. *Guitar World* ranked it as the No. 44 greatest solo of all time and No. 26 on *Total Guitar's* "100 Hottest Guitar Solos." But Mike did not intend to record such an extended and ambitious solo. Producer Tim Palmer encouraged him to pull out all the stops and launch an old-school solo. Then Palmer pasted together the best bits from different takes to create what he thought should be the final version. However, Mike was unhappy with it and decided to give it one last go. As Palmer remembered, "He got it right away. There was no piecing together to do; it was one take." Mike, meanwhile, has always been modest about his fantastic solo. As he explains it, "I copied Ace Frehley's solo from 'She,' which was copied from Robby Krieger's solo in The Doors' 'Five to One.'" While the solo is similar to both, I think you will agree Mike's is better than either.

- The video for "Jeremy" was an absolute sensation on MTV, and they played it on extremely heavy rotation. However, after the horrifying shooting at Columbine High School in 1999, the video was hardly ever shown there again. It was one of those rare intersections of art and popular culture, portraying the lead-up to a school shooting in chilling detail. *Entertainment Weekly* accurately summed up the experience of watching it as "an *Afterschool Special* from hell. When Eddie Vedder yowls the lyric 'Jeremy spoke in class today,' a chill frosts your cranium to the point of queasy enjoyment." At the end of the video, the boy in the video puts the gun in his mouth and pulls the trigger. However, MTV did not show that part due to limitations on displaying graphically violent images.

- Pearl Jam considered the video for "Jeremy" to be TOO successful. The members were concerned that the unforgettable images would overpower the music. Jeff explained, "Ten years from now, I don't want people to remember our songs as videos." The band did not release another video until 1998.

42

- Mike and Eddie admit that they did not have much control over the band's direction when *Ten* was recorded. Stone and Jeff had played together in Green River and Mother Love Bone and knew precisely what they wanted the band to sound like. McCready said that "*Ten* was mostly Stone and Jeff; me and Eddie were along for the ride at that time." Meanwhile, Jeff said, "We knew we were still a long way from being a real band at that point."

CHAPTER 5:

COMMERCIAL PEAK AS GRUNGE SUPERSTARS

1. Pearl Jam was part of an incredible lineup for Lollapalooza 1992. Which of these bands did NOT play with them on that tour?

    a. Cypress Hill
    b. Soundgarden
    c. Rage Against the Machine
    d. Smashing Pumpkins

2. When Eddie, Jeff, and Stone appeared in the movie *Singles*, they were members of what fictional band?

    a. Citizen Dick
    b. Sweet Children
    c. The Obelisk
    d. Atomic Mass

3. True or False: Pearl Jam was near the bottom of the bill at Lollapalooza 1992.

4. How much time elapsed between the release of *Ten* and the release of its follow-up *Vs.*?

a. A year
b. A year and a half
c. More than two years
d. More than three years

5. *Vs.* was a smash hit, breaking the record for most records sold in the first week of release. How long did the band hold on to that record?

    a. Five years
    b. Ten years
    c. Twenty years
    d. They still hold it

6. *Vs.* was primarily recorded in what California town?

    a. Ferndale
    b. Ojai
    c. Nicasio
    d. St. Helena

7. True or False: Eddie had trouble getting inspired in that lovely California town. Therefore, he started to sleep in his truck to feel uncomfortable and break out of the rut.

8. "Glorified G" was a vehemently anti-gun song. What inspired the band to write it?

    a. A drive-by shooting in the news
    b. A mass school shooting
    c. An NRA rally
    d. A band member buying guns

9. Who wrote the music to the song "Go"?

    a. Jeff Ament
    b. Eddie Vedder
    c. Dave Abbruzzese
    d. Mick McCready

10. *Vs.* got generally favorable reviews, despite being a change of direction from *Ten*. Which of the following media outlets was the only one to bash it?

    a. *The New York Times*
    b. *Rolling Stone*
    c. *The Village Voice*
    d. *Entertainment Weekly*

11. Pearl Jam avoided videos for "Vs.," but they released quite a few singles. Which of these was the most successful single from the album?

    a. "Daughter"
    b. "Animal"
    c. "Dissident"
    d. "Go"

12. What is the animal on the cover of *Vs.*?

    a. A Boer Goat
    b. An Angora Goat
    c. A Fainting Goat
    d. A Nigerian Dwarf Goat

13. *Vs.* was not the original name for the album. Which name did they want to use initially?

a. *Five Against One*
b. *Preponderance*
c. *The Jive Five*
d. *Wayward Momentum*

14. When Eddie appeared on the cover of *Time Magazine,* what was the title on the cover?

    a. "The Voice of a Generation"
    b. "Alienation Hits the Mainstream"
    c. "All the Rage"
    d. "Big Anger is Big Money"

15. Why did Eddie agree to do a cover story for *Time*?

    a. He wanted people to understand his music
    b. He wanted to end the beef with Nirvana
    c. He was finally ready to embrace stardom
    d. He didn't agree

16. When Kurt Cobain committed suicide, what was the band doing?

    a. Recording *Vs.*
    b. Mixing *Vs.*
    c. Touring behind *Vs.*
    d. Recording *Vitalogy*

17. True or False: The album *Vs.* sold more than all the other records on the *Billboard* top ten combined in its first week.

18. Which song from *Vs.* did Pearl Jam perform on the MTV music awards?

a. "Go"
b. "Animal"
c. "Dissident"
d. "Rearviewmirror"

19. True or False: "Glorified G" charted even though it was never released as a single.

20. Which song was so difficult for Dave to record that he punched through a snare drum, and then proceeded to throw it off a cliff?

    a. "Rearviewmirror"
    b. "Rats"
    c. "Glorified G"
    d. "Animal"

ANSWERS

1. Smashing Pumpkins

2. Citizen Dick: if you wonder what the others are, they are Green Day, the Cure, and Def Leppard's original names.

3. True: Jeff explained, "A couple of weeks before the tour, there was an opportunity for us to renegotiate, not just the money, but the time slot. But we were like, 'Nah, we don't want any added pressure to this situation.'" He added, "We still have an absolute blast playing shows, but I don't know that we've ever had more fun on tour."

4. More than two years. *Ten* was released on August 27, 1991. Meanwhile, *Vs.* came out on October 19, 1993.

5. Five years: their record was broken by Garth Brooks and his live album *Double Live*.

6. Nicasio: new drummer Dave Abbruzzese called the area "paradise." Eddie wasn't impressed and said, "I fucking hate it here... I've had a hard time... How do you make a rock record here?"

7. True: Eddie hated everything about making that second album. He once said, "The second record, that was the one I enjoyed making the least... I just

didn't feel comfortable in the place we were at because it was very comfortable. I didn't like that at all."

8. A band member buying guns: Dave Abbruzzese bought two firearms during the recording, which did not please Eddie. Dave recalls that "Eddie went, 'Whaaaat, you bought a GUN?' And I said, 'In fact, I bought two,' which ended up as the song's opening line. I think it's fair to say Eddie was pretty outraged."

9. C- Dave Abbruzzese: Mike says that Dave is "a hell of a guitar player. I remember he wrote 'Go' on an acoustic, without a pick."

10. C- *Village Voice*: the snobby Robert Thomas Christgau rated the album a dud.

11. "Daughter": it reached No. 79 on the *Billboard* Hot 100 and topped the Mainstream Rock and Alternative Airplay charts.

12. An Angora Goat: Jeff took the picture in Victor, Montana. He said it represented their feeling of being trapped by expectation and stardom.

13. *Five Against One*: some of the initial pressings of the album has that name. Others do not have any name or artwork on them. Jeff said both versions of the name reflected the internal dynamic of the band. "For me, that title represented a lot of the struggles that you go through to make a record. Your own

independence -- your own soul -- versus everybody else's. In this band, and I think in rock in general, the art of compromise is almost as important as the art of individual expression. You might have five great artists in the band, but if they can't compromise and work together, you don't have a great band."

14. "All the Rage": it continued: Angry young rockers like PEARL JAM give voice to the passions and fears of a generation.

15. He didn't agree: Pearl Jam had no interest in more media exposure at that time and did not cooperate. *Time* used an image of Eddie anyway.

16. Touring behind *Vs.*: the band played a show three nights later in Fairfax, Virginia. Eddie said, "I don't think any of us would be in this room tonight if it weren't for Kurt Cobain." The band considered canceling the rest of the tour but decided not to."

17. True.

18. B- "Animal": MTV rarely allows a song without a video to be played at their awards, but Pearl Jam was too big to pass up at that time.

19. True. It reached No. 39 on the mainstream rock charts anyway.

20. "Rearviewmirror": Dave felt that producer Brendan O'Brien was subjecting him to too much pressure on that song.

DID YOU KNOW?

- Lollapalooza 1992 was a massive cultural and musical shift. It was the moment where alternative music stepped out of the shadows and into the mainstream. For Pearl Jam and Soundgarden's members, it was a fantastic moment of vindication for their musical direction. Chris Cornell recalled, "I think it was one of my favorite tours of my career because we shared a lot of camaraderie. It's like your buddies you grew up with that you played in front of ten people with for years, and now you're on tour together playing for twenty-five thousand people. And it seems to mean something culturally." The closeness indeed showed. When Eddie missed the bus, Chris was about to fill in as a guest Pearl Jam singer. However, Eddie made it JUST in time when Chris and the band were already onstage. He had successfully hitchhiked to the show. With massive smiles on their faces, they played "Hunger Strike" together.

- When they recorded *Vs.*, the band made a concentrated and intentional effort to act as a cohesive group. Rather than have Stone and Jeff bring many written songs as they had on *Ten*, the songs were developed through organic jam sessions. Stone explained, "I think we allowed things to develop in a more natural, band-oriented sort of way, rather than me bringing in a bunch of stuff that was already arranged." Gossard added that most of the songs were arranged once Vedder joined in and started singing, elaborating, "You could tell when the music wanted to change just by the way he was singing."

- Pearl Jam and Nirvana were the two biggest bands to emerge from the Seattle scene. However, they were pretty different. Nirvana was highly committed to the punk rock aesthetic and saw themselves as heirs to bands like Sonic Youth and the Melvins. Meanwhile, Pearl Jam was part of the alternative scene but was heavily influenced by classic rock. Therefore, Nirvana developed a particular distaste for Pearl Jam. Cobain famously said that Pearl Jam was a bunch of "careerists" and only in it for the money. Kurt's wife, Courtney Love, said, "I remember when Pearl Jam beat Nirvana onto the cover of *Time*, and that pissed Kurt off, let me tell you." However, their relationship ended on a good note. To Eddie's credit, he refused to get sucked into the rivalry and never said a bad word about Nirvana. When asked about Pearl Jam, later on, Kurt said, "I'm not going to do that anymore. It hurts Eddie, and he's a good guy." The truth is, Eddie and Kurt had a lot in common. Both were alienated high-school kids who found refuge in music and superstardom by expressing their inner pain.

- The song "Daughter" was clearly written about a dysfunctional mother-daughter relationship. However, it also had another theme. The girl in the song suffered from a learning disability, and Eddie was trying to draw awareness to the topic. Eddie told Melody Maker, "It's only in the last few years that they've actually been able to diagnose these learning disabilities that before were looked at as misbehavior, as just outright rebelliousness. But no one knew what it was. And these kids, because they seemed unable or reluctant to learn, they'd end up getting the shit beaten outta them. The song ends, you know, with this idea of the shades going down -- so that the neighbors can't see what happens next."

- The background and theme of *Vs.* was the alienation Pearl Jam felt at their massive success. The expectations from Eddie to follow up *Ten* were enormous, and he had a challenging time recording the album. He found stardom incredibly difficult to deal with, as he explained, "I don't want to be a star, it's not worth it, to have my picture taken and have my face everywhere. It's scary; it scares me. I could scare a lot of people with my face! I personally think that the less you know about a musician, the better. All that you need is the music, and then you won't have any other preconceptions." It wasn't just Eddie who was frustrated. Jeff says the band felt like they were "slaves" to fame and the record company. Therefore, the band pursued a rawer and more uncompromising sound than on their debut. They avoided sounding like *Ten* and refused to release music videos. Nonetheless, the album was a smash hit.

CHAPTER 6:

VITALOGY AND THE WAR AGAINST TICKETMASTER

1. What event started Pearl Jam's decision to take on Ticketmaster?
    a. Ticketmaster overcharged for fan club special tickets
    b. Ticketmaster put a service charge on a free concert
    c. Ticketmaster charged the band for their shows
    d. Ticketmaster raised their rates

2. Which big band joined Pearl Jam in their struggle against Ticketmaster?
    a. R.E.M.
    b. U2
    c. Metallica
    d. No one

3. As they began to change their policy on concert tickets, Pearl Jam lowered all tickets' prices to their show to $18. How much did the band lose by doing so?

a. 1 million dollars
b. 2 million dollars
c. 3 million dollars
d. 4 million dollars

4. In 1994, Pearl Jam insisted that Ticketmaster charge only $1.80 service charge on tickets to their shows. Meanwhile, Ticketmaster would not work for less than $4. What ended up happening?

a. Pearl Jam caved
b. Ticketmaster caved
c. The two sides compromised
d. The tour was canceled

5. Pearl Jam's next tour, the *Vitalogy* tour, faced a lot of cancellations. Why?

a. They couldn't find non-Ticketmaster venues
b. Ticketmaster arranged a boycott against them
c. The band succumbed to infighting
d. Eddie suffered severe food poisoning

6. Pearl Jam's complaints about Ticketmaster led to a Justice Department investigation against the company on suspicion of breaking anti-trust laws. What happened to that investigation?

a. It was closed with no results
b. Ticketmaster was fined
c. Ticketmaster was forced to change its prices
d. Ticketmaster was forced to change its business practices

7. Many years later, Ticketmaster engaged in its own battle with third-party ticket sales sites like StubHub. Which side did Pearl Jam take on this issue in 2020?

    a. The third-party websites' side
    b. Ticketmaster's side
    c. They remained neutral
    d. They refused to work with either

8. How did Pearl Jam write the songs for *Vitalogy*?

    a. Most of the songs were outtakes from previous sessions
    b. They wrote most of the songs on the road
    c. They wrote most of the songs in the studio
    d. They wrote the songs separately before the sessions

9. *Vitalogy* was recorded in several locations. Which of these cities was NOT the site of a Pearl Jam recording session for their third album?

    a. Atlanta
    b. New York
    c. New Orleans
    d. Seattle

10. Which song on *Vitalogy* was initially played by Eddie's former band Bad Radio?

    a. "Last Exit"
    b. "Corduroy"
    c. "Better Man"

d. "Immortality"

11. Mike recorded the song "Not for You" with a beautiful twelve-string Rickenbacker. Which guitar legend gifted Mike that guitar as a Christmas present?

    a. Roger McGuinn
    b. Tom Petty
    c. Peter Buck
    d. George Harrison

12. "Spin the Black Circle" is probably Pearl Jam's fastest song. Whose idea was it to play it like that?

    a. Eddie
    b. Stone
    c. Jeff
    d. Mike

13. True or False: *Vitalogy* was, at the time, the second fastest-selling album of all-time behind *Vs.*?

14. Dave was kicked out of the band over personal conflicts with other members. Who did he have trouble getting along with?

    a. Eddie and Jeff
    b. Mike and Stone
    c. Jeff and Mike
    d. Eddie and Mike

15. True or False: Jack Irons came in and finished all of the drum parts Dave did not do on *Vitalogy*.

16. True or False: *Vitalogy* was, at first, only released on vinyl. It remains the highest-selling new vinyl record released since 1991.

17. What was the original name of the album *Vitalogy* before the band (again) changed it at the last minute?

    a. *Life*
    b. *Death*
    c. *Wisdom*
    d. *Courage*

18. The packaging for *Vitalogy* contains what?

    a. Personal photos from the band
    b. Sections of an outdated medical textbook
    c. Jeff's art
    d. Surreal landscape pictures

19. The song "Hard to Imagine" was rejected from the album. However, it later appeared in a 1998 feature film. Which movie was it?

    a. *Chicago Cab*
    b. *Smoke Signals*
    c. *Pleasantville*
    d. *Rushmore*

20. Who was the unlikely inspiration for the song "Corduroy"?

    a. Celine Dion
    b. Gloria Estefan

c. Ricky Martin
d. Bryan Adams

ANSWERS

1. B- Ticketmaster put a service charge on a free concert. Understandably, the band felt that kind of defeated the purpose.

2. No one. R.E.M.'s manager testified with them in court, but no one joined the boycott.

3. B- 2 million dollars: they also lowered the costs of all t-shirts.

4. The tour was canceled. The band lost around 3 million dollars on that.

5. Eddie suffered severe food poisoning. In a show before 50,000 people at Golden Gate Park in San Francisco, Neil Young had to step in on vocals.

6. It was closed with no results. The Justice Department announced that Ticketmaster was not breaking anti-trust laws.

7. Pearl Jam entirely took Ticketmaster's side and has worked to make sure tickets to the Gigaton tour are not available on third-party websites. So, fans that wanted to buy tickets presale had to sign up for Ticketmaster's SafeTix service. Oh, how times have changed.

8. They wrote most of the songs on the road. The songs were written during the *Vs.* tour. They even

began to perform some of them regularly before recording.

9. New York: the album was recorded in the Bad Animals studio in Seattle, Southern Tracks and Doppler in Atlanta, and Kingsway in New Orleans.

10. "Better Man": The band considered releasing the song on *Vs.* but decided not to because it seemed too mainstream and accessible. However, producer Brendan O'Brien insisted it was a "blatantly great pop song," and the band recorded it. It was an instant classic.

11. B- Tom Petty: Mike would later cover "Tom's Won't Back Down" with KT Tunstall and Thunderpussy bassist Leah Julius for charity.

12. Eddie: he took an original take and sped it up and asked the band to play it like that. Jeff was not happy. He later laughed, "I was like, 'Ugh... I can't play the entire Dead Kennedys' back catalog!' I didn't really want to make music like that at the time." Mike has admitted that he has trouble keeping up when they play it live.

13. True: it sold 877,000 copies in the first week after its release in the US.

14. Eddie and Jeff: Stone recalled that "On a superficial level, it was a political struggle: For whatever reason, his ability to communicate with Ed and Jeff

was very stifled. I certainly don't think it was all Dave Abbruzzese's fault that it was stifled."

15. False: session drummers and drumming techs recorded quite a few parts. Drum tech Jimmy Shoaf played the drum part on "Satan's Bed." Jack only played on "Hey Foxymophandlemama, That's Me."

16. False: *Vitalogy* was the highest-selling vinyl album in the post-record era for almost two decades. But Jack White broke the record (pardon the pun) with his 2014 release *Lazaretto*.

17. *Life*: the first single from the album, *Spin the Black Circle* says it is from the album *Life*.

18. Sections of an outdated medical textbook. Eddie found the book at a garage sale. The band later discovered that some of the books were still copyrighted.

19. *Chicago Cab*: Stone Gossard's label put out the soundtrack.

20. Ricky Martin: As Eddie tells it, he had a cheap corduroy jacket that he bought for $12, and it was being resold for $650. As the singer said to the AV club, "The ultimate one as far as being co-opted was that there was a guy on TV, predictably patterned, I guess, after the way I was looking those days, with long hair and an Army T-shirt. They put this new character on a soap opera, so there was a guy, more handsome than I, parading around on *General*

Hospital. And the funny thing is, that guy was Ricky Martin."

DID YOU KNOW?

- Pearl Jam found that trying to organize a tour without Ticketmaster was a nightmare. The band had to organize every detail about the shows, from the fences to the toilets. Eddie remembers, "We were having week-long meetings about chain-link fences and porta-potties. And because we would only play in non-Ticketmaster venues, we had to go to these really out-of-the-way places. Mike said, "We had to handle everything ourselves. I remember taking calls about portaloos. It was an ordeal." At the end of the day, it is not surprising that Pearl Jam surrendered so that they could focus on the music.

- Pearl Jam is known for its camaraderie and the strong bonds between the members. However, *Vitalogy* was an exception to this rule. While Stone had been the driving force in the band in its early years, he was being shunted aside by Eddie. As Gossard withdrew emotionally, the band sorely missed his ability to resolve their conflicts. Stone has since accepted that his role in the band has diminished. He said, "If it had always remained my band, my natural tendency would have been to get more complex and arrange things more and more. That wouldn't necessarily be good for Eddie or anyone else in the band. Of course, I enjoy being self-indulgent. [laughs] And I look forward to the time when I can become more indulgent with my songwriting. But this band is a family, and it's a process that we have to grow with together."

- If so, following the recording of *Vitalogy*, Eddie was the undisputed leader of the band. As Stone explained, "There's no getting around the fact that Eddie is the man. As far as emotional and spiritual energy goes, he *IS* the leader of this band." However, he maintains control over the band by being reasonable and listening to the other members. Therefore, Stone says, "Eddie can listen to reason; Eddie can be swayed or talked in or out of certain things. Eddie allows other people to lead in this band and to have certain roles that are very fundamental to the decision-making process."

- As if the band did not have enough trouble, between Stone and Eddie's power struggle and Dave being kicked out of the band, Mike struggled with substance abuse. He was abusing both alcohol and cocaine, ending up in rehab. Stone explained that "Mike's a pretty awful drunk. Not that he got malicious or mean openly to people, but he would get out of control consistently. It was a difficult situation where you could find yourself blaming Mike for a lot of your own frustrations with the band when he was f--ked up or couldn't come to practice. And we're used to loving Mike and knowing how much fun and how talented he is. I got upset that he might throw away a great opportunity to be in a cool band and work it out. He decided to go into treatment, and everyone was thrilled. How could you not be? Here was Mike taking responsibility for himself and his own happiness, going to a new level." Thankfully, rehab worked, and Mike has remained a vital part of the band.

• Unlike the first two albums, *Vitalogy* got fairly mixed reviews. Some, like *Newsday*, didn't like its general punk rock feel. Others, such as the reviewer for *Time* magazine, didn't appreciate the stranger experimental moments on it. However, some reviewers who felt the band's early material was too commercial were won over by the new approach. The *L.A. Times* critic quipped, "This isn't just the best Pearl Jam album, but a better album than the band once even seemed capable of making." Meanwhile, their former nemesis from the *Village Voice*, Robert Christgau, praised the band. He noted that "three or four of these songs are faster and riffier than anything else in P. Jam's book, token experiments like 'Bugs' are genuinely weird, and in an era of compulsory irony [Vedder's] sincerity is something like a relief."

CHAPTER 7:

GAINING INDEPENDENCE ON *MIRRORBALL* AND *NO CODE*

1. During the early 1990s, bands like Pearl Jam and Nirvana expressed a lot of respect for Neil Young. As a result, he was called what?

    a. The Godfather of Grunge
    b. The King of Grunge
    c. The Grungy Duke
    d. El Grungo

2. When Pearl Jam played with Neil on the MTV Awards show, which song did they play?

    a. "Heart of Gold"
    b. "Like a Hurricane"
    c. "Rockin' in the Free World"
    d. "Hey Hey, My My"

3. How many of the songs on Neil Young's *Mirrorball* were co-written by Pearl Jam?

    a. None
    b. Three

    c. Five
    d. All of them

4. When the *Neil Young News* blog asked fans to rate the best Neil Young recorded shows, what place did his show with Pearl Jam in Dublin from 1995 take?

    a. First place
    b. Second place
    c. Third place
    d. Fourth place

5. How many US shows did Neil Young play with Pearl Jam in support of the album?

    a. None
    b. Ten
    c. Fifteen
    d. Twenty

6. While the rest of the band toured with Neil Young, Eddie worked on a soundtrack. Which 1995 movie was it for?

    a. The Quick and the Dead
    b. Dead Man Walking
    c. Crimson Tide
    d. Congo

7. Pearl Jam has an excellent outtake from the *Mirrorball* sessions called "I Got Id." The song is sometimes called what instead?

a. "I Got Fucked"
b. "I Got Shit"
c. "I Got Ass"
d. "I Got Drugs"

8. True or False: Brendan O'Brien produced all the tracks on *Mirrorball* and its companion E.P. "Merkin Ball."

9. How long after Eddie suffered his terrible food poisoning did the band begin to work on No Code?

a. Three weeks later
b. A month later
c. Two months later
d. Twenty-one weeks later

10. Which band member was initially not invited to the recording sessions due to internal squabbling?

a. Mike
b. Stone
c. Jeff
d. Jack

11. Which song on *No Code* features an electric sitar?

a. "In My Tree"
b. "Habit"
c. "Off He Goes"
d. "Who You Are"

12. Which song on the album was about Eddie's horrible experience with a stalker?

a. "Habit"
b. "Lukin"
c. "Present Tense"
d. "Mankind"

13. Who sings lead vocals on the song "Mankind"?

    a. Jeff
    b. Eddie
    c. Stone
    d. Jack

14. Which song on *No Code* was about Eddie's food poisoning episode?

    a. "Hail Hail"
    b. "Red Mosquito"
    c. "I'm Open"
    d. "Habit"

15. After the initial sessions in Chicago and New Orleans, the band finished the album at the Seattle Studio Litho. Which member of the band owns that studio?

    a. Eddie
    b. Jeff
    c. Mike
    d. Stone

16. The band played *No Code* in its entirety only once. What year was it?

    a. 1997
    b. 2007

c. 2009

d. 2014

17. Where did No Code debut on the *Billboard* Top 200 charts?

   a. No. 1

   b. No. 7

   c. No. 32

   d. No. 41

18. The cover of *No Code* features 156 Polaroids. One of them belongs to an NBA player. Who is it?

   a. Mookie Blaylock

   b. Dennis Rodman

   c. Hakeem Olajuwon

   d. Charles Barkley

19. True or False: The song "Off He Goes" seems to be about an unreliable friend. However, Eddie wrote it about himself.

20. True or False: The band recorded a song called Olympic Platinum, inspired by the 1996 Summer Olympics held in Atlanta.

ANSWERS

1. A- The Godfather of Grunge

2. C- "Rockin' in the Free World"

3. A- None: "Peace and Love" was co-written with Eddie. The rest of the band did not get any credits.

4. A- First place

5. A- None because of the Ticketmaster affair. However, I got to see them in Europe, and it was unforgettable.

6. B- *Dead Man Walking*: Eddie recorded a duet with famous Qawwali singer Nusrat Fateh Ali Khan.

7. B- "I Got Shit": when he introduced the song at a 1998 show, Eddie said, "Neil gave me a songwriting lesson at a half-price rate; this is what I came up with...on my final, he gave me a B+ I think."

8. False: Brendan produced Mirrorball, but Brett Eliason produced Merkin Ball. However, Brendan does play base on I Go Id, one of the songs on Merkin Ball.

9. A- Three weeks later:not long after a somewhat traumatic experience, where the band was booed in San Francisco after Eddie was forced to abandon the show.

10. C- Jeff: even when he got there, Jeff was not getting along with the other members. "I feel like I had all these ideas that I wanted to contribute, and people just weren't interested," Ament said in 2003. "Luckily, I had a home studio, and I was doing a lot of recording on my own. If it wouldn't have been for that, I doubt I would've stayed in the band."

11. D- "Who You Are": the song also had a distinctive polyrhythmic drum pattern. "I'd been playing that [drum pattern] since I was eight," Irons said at the time. "It was inspired by a Max Roach drum solo I heard at a drum shop when I was a little kid." It was quite a departure from the usual Pearl Jam sound.

12. B- "Lukin": the chilling lyrics to the rage-filled song include the lines, "I find my wife, I call the cops, this day's work's never done. The last I heard that freak was purchasing a fucking gun." The song is called "Lukin" because Eddie would hide out at Mudhoney/Melvins bassist Matt Lukin's home during this episode. Matt recalled, "The Pearl Jam song 'Lukin' is about how my kitchen's a sanctuary for him. Also, I was giving him shit about all their songs being too long. That inspired him to make 'Lukin' a one-minute song. I've always flipped him shit. Never let him be the rock star that he is."

13. C- Stone: Eddie sings background vocals on the track. It is the only album track on which Eddie

does not sing lead vocals. There are a few B-sides with lead vocals by other members. Gossard was not feeling particularly happy with his role in the band at the time. As he later recalled, "I think I probably just recorded it with Jack Irons maybe trying to do the demo or whatever, and I didn't know whether it was going to make it on the record or not. At that time, I was feeling very frustrated, and I wasn't feeling as connected to the songwriting process as I did, obviously, on the first two records. It was a time where the experimental gloves had come out, and if we were going to experiment, I was going to experiment, too. So that was my experiment, that I could write a pop song and I could sing it, and it could be halfway legit."

14. B- "Red Mosquito": when introducing the song, Eddie explained, "Alright, this one goes back a way. It's all about... uh... being trapped in a hotel room with an insect." He would later explain, "That whole [Golden Gate Park] thing was a blur based on some bad food. It was really, really bad. Looking back at it, it doesn't seem as intense as it was, but it was horrible. I just felt not human, and looking back, I should have got through that show somehow, and I think the fact that Neil [Young] was there made me feel like I could get off the hook in some way, and I did go out for a few songs. I just didn't feel good about the whole thing. I felt swallowed up by the whole deal. It was just a

situation where you couldn't go to work. But I think now I'd probably get through that show."

15. D- Stone: Stone established the studio in 1995. It has been used by Mastodon, the Dave Matthews Band, the Deftones, Soundgarden, and many other bands.

16. D- 2014: it was one of the highest-selling bootleg releases in Pearl Jam history and the most popular for that tour.

17. A- No. 1: however, it quickly started to fall and did not sell as much as the first three albums. In fact, none of their future albums ever did.

18. B- Dennis Rodman: he was a friend of the band.

19. True: during a performance in Katowice, Poland, Eddie introduced the song, saying that "this is about being friends with an asshole" while pointing at himself. In an interview, he said it's about how "I'll show up, and everything's great and then all of a sudden I'm outta there."

20. True: the song was written by *No Code* mixer Nick Didia. It was released as a single only available to fan club members on Christmas.

DID YOU KNOW?

- With Pearl Jam playing as the backing band, the Neil Young album *Mirrorball* was completed very quickly. They had come up with the idea to work together in mid-January 1995 and completed recording by early February. The spontaneous nature of Neil's work is reflected in his approach to recording. Mike said, "He's laid back. We'd get together, do a couple, three takes of each song, then move on. It was very spontaneous." Aside from two songs, every one of the pieces on the album was written the day before the recording. Neil said it was very natural to just play with Pearl Jam. Neil said, "There was no direction. I just played my songs the way I would play them with anybody else. I played them like I was sure everything was going to be there. It was evident to me right away they were going to be able to deliver the goods. They picked things up real well. I'm fortunate to have these great musicians – them and Crazy Horse – to play with."

- Eddie has one of the most terrifying stalker stories of any celebrity out there. In 1996, a woman drove her car into his house's outer walls, driving fifty miles per hour. The woman bombarded Eddie with letters for months. In the letters, she accused the singer of having raped her and fathering both her children. Oh, she also thought Eddie was Jesus, and she wrote in her letters, "Jesus rapes." The stalker nearly died in the crash and ended up in prison. The experience scarred Vedder, who was known for being very open with his fans until then. The singer famously gave his phone number to fans experiencing pain in their private lives. However, after that experience, Eddie understandably had twenty-four-hour security for several years. Eddie later explained, "One of the reasons you're protecting yourself is because you've been forthcoming with your emotions," he says. "So, you have to build a wall. And now people are driving into the wall. That's what fucks with your head. I felt like my brain was a whore, and I was getting mindfucked."

- Pearl Jam picked an awful time to record *No Code* in Chicago. That summer, 739 people in the city died from the intense heat. Most of the victims were vulnerable elderly who could not afford to air condition. The heat was made worse by the urban conditions in many areas of the city, which trap high temperature and raise it by a few crucial degrees. With Eddie still reeling from his food poisoning, and Jeff at odds with the band, the recording process started badly. However, the band regained its cohesion—the members credit drummer Jack Irons for keeping them together.

The drummer was more settled than the rest of the band. He had a wife and children and had seen much worse band trouble in the past as a member of the Red Hot Chili Peppers. He urged everyone to talk about their problems. Mike called him "a big spiritual influence, if not the biggest." By the time the sessions were done, O'Brien recalls, "It was really a transitional record. We had a good time making it."

- The band could not tour in big venues behind *No Code* because of the still ongoing Ticketmaster mess. Therefore, they played in some pretty out-of-the-way places in the short tour they performed in support of the album. One of those shows was played at Downing Stadium, a somewhat run-down establishment on New York's Randall's Island. Many fans consider it to be the greatest show the band ever played. For some reason, in the middle of the show, Vedder wrapped himself in duct tape and said, "The best way to change something is to change yourself. Only you know who you are. No one can tell you who you are. No one can tell me who I am." The show is considered in retrospect to be a declaration that Pearl Jam is no longer going to try to be the most prominent or most influential band. It would play what it wanted, when it wanted, for a core audience that followed them no matter what.

- There is no other way to put it: *No Code* was a commercial flop by their previous albums' standards. It debuted at No. 1 like all of their previous albums but sold 366,500 copies, around 200,000 less than projected. It was eventually certified platinum, but in comparison with the first three releases' multi-platinum performances, that was considered a failure. It also received some mixed reviews, notably from the *New York Times*, which complained that as far as the songs are concerned, "about half are worth the effort." Meanwhile, *Entertainment Weekly* complained that it "becomes a collection of fragments that don't add up to much of anything, except a portrait of a musically disjointed band." Luckily, Rolling Stone understood the album better. As critic David Fricke wrote, *No Code* is "abrupt in its mood swings almost to the point of vertigo." He praised the album as "the kind of impulsive, quixotic, provocative ruckus that has become rare in a modern-rock mainstream" and added that "*No Code* basically means no rule books, no limits and, above all, no fear." Exactly, David.

CHAPTER 8:

YIELD

1. The songs on *Yield* were written more democratically than on the last two albums. Why did Eddie write fewer songs on his own this time around?

    a. His songs were not good
    b. Other band members threatened to quit unless things changed
    c. Producer Brendan O'Brien asked for a different process
    d. Eddie asked to write less

2. Which song on *Yield* was inspired by Mikhail Bulgakov's masterful novel *The Master and Margarita*?

    a. "Pilate"
    b. "Do the Evolution"
    c. "No Way"
    d. "Given to Fly"

3. Which member of the band does not play on "Do the Evolution"?

a. Stone
b. Mike
c. Matt
d. Jeff

4. "Do the Evolution" had the first music video Pearl Jam released since *Ten*. Which studio was responsible for the stunning animation?

    a. Epoch Ink Animation
    b. Pixomondo
    c. Animal Logic
    d. Aardman Animations

5. True or False: In 2020, an entire book on the video for "Do the Evolution" was published.

6. The director of the "Do the Evolution" video also directed what other 1990s landmark video?

    a. Daft Punk – "Around the World"
    b. Blind Melon – "No Rain"
    c. Korn – "Freak on a Leash"
    d. Nine Inch Nails – "Closer"

7. Mike wrote the song "Given to Fly" in one day and the riff to Faithfull. What happened that day?

    a. Someone close to him died
    b. It was an anniversary of going clean
    c. He was snowed in
    d. He realized he had to come up with material for the album

8. True or False: The song "Wishlist" was originally eight minutes long and had many more wishes, which Eddie cut for the final version.

9. Jeff was much happier with his role in songwriting on *Yield*. How many of the songs he wrote appeared on the album?

   a. Two
   b. Four
   c. Five
   d. Six

10. Where did Yield debut in the charts?

   a. No. 2
   b. No. 6
   c. No. 12
   d. No. 14

11. What was the documentary on the making of *Yield* called?

   a. *Yield Congealed*
   b. *I Stopped Trying to Make a Difference*
   c. *The One-Video Theory*
   d. *Low Lights and High Lights*

12. True or False: Pearl Jam had their shortest European tour yet promoting *Yield*.

13. Which band played the most gigs as a supporting act on the *Yield* tour?

   a. Mudhoney

b. Tenacious D

c. Spacehog

d. Iggy Pop

14. How many shows did Jack play drums on during the *Yield* tour before being replaced by Matt Cameron?

    a. None

    b. Ten

    c. Twenty

    d. All of them

15. During the *Yield* tour, the fans began a campaign asking the band to reintroduce a long-neglected song and play it. The band finally caved and played the song during a show at Madison Square Garden in 1998. What song was it?

    a. "Long Road"

    b. "Out of My Mind"

    c. "Bee Girl"

    d. "Breath"

16. Which *Yield* song was the most successful on the *Billboard* charts?

    a. "Do the Evolution"

    b. "Faithless"

    c. "Given to Fly"

    d. "Wishlist"

17. The live album *Live on Two Legs* ends with a cover of what Neil Young song?

a. "Fuckin' Up"
b. "Rockin' in the Free World"
c. "Like an Inca"
d. "Sleeps with Angels"

18. Which are the only two songs from *Ten* to appear on *Live on Two Legs*?

    a. "Black" and "Jeremy"
    b. "Jeremy" and "Even Flow"
    c. "Black" and "Even Flow"
    d. "Porch" and "Black"

19. True or False: *Live on Two Legs* was the first of over two hundred live albums released by the band.

20. True or False: *Live on Two Legs* went platinum.

ANSWERS

1. D- Eddie asked to write less. He made a concentrated effort to encourage other members to write. The singer felt burned out from carrying too much of the load and wanted a better dynamic in the band. It worked. Mike said, "I used to be afraid of him and not want to confront him on things... We talk more now, and hang out... He seems very, very centered now."

2. A- "Pilate": Jeff explained, "I think 'Pilate' was the question I was asking myself, and 'Low Light' was the answer, the realization. Have you ever read The Master and Margarita? I just read that book, and at the end, they talk about Pontius Pilate being all alone on a mountain with his dog. He couldn't sleep, and he couldn't function. It really struck me hard because, at that point, I was feeling very alone. I've always had this recurring dream about being old and just me and my dog sitting on the porch. It wasn't necessarily a sad dream or a premonition, but it did get me to thinking about why Pilate was so alone and freaked out."

3. D- Jeff: Stone played the bass on that song.

4. A- Epoch Ink Animation

5. True: The book is called *Pearl Jam: Art of Do The Evolution* and was published by IDW Publishing.

6. Korn – "Freak on a Leash"

7. C- He was snowed in. Mike says, "It was snowing here in Seattle, which it rarely does, and so they shut down all the streets, and I couldn't get my car out of the driveway. And I have a Volvo, and you'd think those would be able to drive in the snow, but no, it wasn't going anywhere, so I was kind of stuck in my condo. And I wrote that riff [for 'Given to Fly'] and the 'Faithfull' riff that day."

8. True: when Pearl Jam performs the song live, Eddie will often pull out some of the wishes to cut or add new ones.

9. A- Two: He wrote "Pilate" and "Low Light"

10. A- No. 2. It was the first of their albums that did not debut at No. 1.

11. C- *Single Video Theory*: released in 1998, it carefully documents the evolution in songwriting and the changing dynamic between the band members.

12. False: Pearl Jam did not tour Europe at all to promote *Yield*. The tour focused on North America and had a few dates in Australia and New Zealand as well.

13. A- Mudhoney: in case you were wondering, all the other acts opened for Pearl Jam on the *Yield* tour as well.

14. C- Twenty: after shows in Australia and Hawaii, Jack decided it was too much and quit. Therefore, the band had a short time to arrange a replacement. Cameron said, "I got a phone call out of the blue from Mr. Ed Ved, Stoney, and Kelly. I was ambushed. It was really short notice. He called and said, 'Hey, what are you doing this summer?'" Matt played his first show with the band in Missoula, Montana, on June 20, 1998.

15. D- "Breath:" the song originally appeared on the movie *Singles'* soundtrack and struck a chord with hardcore fans. The band was touched by the campaign and has played the song regularly since 1998.

16. C- "Given to Fly": it reached No. 21 on the *Billboard* main chart. It also topped the Mainstream Rock chart and reached No. 3 on the Alternative chart.

17. A- "Fuckin' Up": extra points if you noted that they also do part of "Rockin' in the Free World" during the rendition of "Daughter" on the album.

18. C- "Black" and "Even Flow"

19. False: it was the first of over three hundred live albums released by the band.

20. True: it went platinum in the US, Canada, Australia, and New Zealand.

DID YOU KNOW?

- *Yield* brought the tensions that had been simmering in the band since *Vitalogy* to an end. Jeff and Stone found their place in the band under Eddie's leadership. Jeff says, "Everybody really got a little bit of their say on the record...because of that, everybody feels like they're an integral part of the band." That was part of a generally more positive attitude the band brought into the recording of *Yield*. Eddie said that with the spotlight on Pearl Jam's every move, he could enjoy the creative process more. The singer said, "We're not the same people we were five years ago. There's 'cool' and 'cynical,' which to me is dull and boring. It's a perfect way to get to youth, you know, being sarcastic and saying everything sucks. But at this point, I'd have to fake it to do that." He went on to add, "I'm a little more positive about the whole trip now. We've had time to count some blessings. I'm in a tremendous position, being in a band and making music. I'd be an idiot not to enjoy the opportunity."

- Jack Irons left the band after the recording of *Yield*. The official reason was that touring had proved too strenuous for him, but he has since revealed that his struggle with bipolar disorder led to the decision. "When I left Pearl Jam in '98, I wasn't in a good place," Irons recalls. "Honestly, the way I felt, the last thing on my mind was music. Music is, I believe, something you do when you're feeling strong. I pretty much had to kind of give up my career to get my life together." Touring with Pearl Jam was, indeed, too much. "You've got to be fairly healthy to go play for 15, 20, 30,000 people four or five times a week. You can't start to come unglued. There's thousands and thousands of people counting on you to do your job and to do it well. I just couldn't do it at the time." His contribution to *Yield* and *No Code* was immense. Eddie says, "No one plays like him. There's some kind of wild card, the way he hears things and the way he plays things that's completely his own."

- The North American tour behind *Yield* was the first full-scale tour they had done on the continent in years. The band admitted defeat in their struggle with Ticketmaster and used their services once again. Jack Irons' replacement with Matt Cameron also made it easier to play large concerts since Jack had a mental illness.

- The release of *Yield* signified a significant change in Pearl Jam's attitude. They had spent much of the 90's battling against Ticketmaster. They were also at odds with stardom and increasingly with each other. *Yield* sees the band let go of the mantle it had taken on and the strain the members had put on themselves. Eddie sings, "'I'm not trying to make a difference, I'll stop trying to make a difference" in the song "No Way," hinting at both his rejection of fame and the end of the crusade against Ticketmaster. However, notably, the song was written by Stone rather than Eddie. The song is also cryptic about whether they will take on new causes in the future since Eddie sings "no way" after saying he is done trying to make a difference...

CHAPTER 9:

BINAURAL AND RIOT ACT

1. In 1999, Pearl Jam covered the song "Last Kiss" and had a surprisingly big hit with it. The song was used on a benefit album. What was it benefitting?

    a. Victims of the Salt Lake City tornado
    b. Victims of Hurricane Floyd
    c. Refugees of the Kosovo War
    d. Refugees from the Kargil War

2. True or False: The song "Last Kiss" was based on a true story.

3. "Last Kiss" reached No. 2 on the *Billboard* charts. Which song kept it from reaching No. 1?

    a. "If You Had My Love" – Jennifer Lopez
    b. "What's My Age Again?" – Blink 182
    c. "Every Morning" – Sugar Ray
    d. "Bills, Bills, Bills" – Destiny's Child

4. The band's sixth album is called *Binaural*, after a recording technique they used in the studio. What does the process involve?

a. The placement of two microphones at an angle of about 110 degrees, with the capsules spaced 17 cm apart
b. Two microphones often arranged on the head of a mannequin
c. Placing one microphone sideways at a 90-degree angle from the instrument, and the other is pointed directly toward the instrument
d. The placement of two microphones at an angle between 90-135 degrees so that their capsules coincide at a single point

5. The cover and artwork of *Binaural* depict what interstellar phenomenon?

a. Gamma-ray bursts
b. Supernovas
c. Red dwarfs
d. Nebulas

6. True or False: During the recording of *Binaural*, Mike once again checked himself into rehab. This time for the over-consumption of prescription drugs.

7. True or False: Danish police released a report saying that Pearl Jam was responsible for the disaster at the Roskilde Festival in 2000.

8. True or False: The Roskilde police continue to blame Pearl Jam for the tragedy.

9. True or False: The band considered breaking up after the Roskilde tragedy.

10. During the *Binaural* tour, the band celebrated ten years from its first live performance. Where did it hold that landmark show?

    a. KeyArena, Seattle
    b. Madison Square Garden, New York
    c. MGM Grand, Las Vegas
    d. Shoreline Amphitheater, Mountain View

11. True or False: The band began issuing the *Official Bootleg* series in 2000 to combat their fans' tendency to make illegal recordings of their shows.

12. True or False: When Pearl Jam released their second set of *Official Bootleg* shows, they broke their own record for the most newly released albums on the chart at one time.

13. Pearl Jam played the America: A Tribute to Heroes benefit concert for the victims of 9/11 with Neil Young. Which song did they play?

    a. "Downtown"
    b. "Long Road"
    c. "Act of Love"
    d. "I'm the Ocean"

14. Who produced the band's seventh album, *Riot Act*?

    a. Brendan O'Brien
    b. Tchad Blake
    c. Adam Kasper

d. Rick Parashar

15. Matt Cameron wrote the lyrics to one of the songs on *Riot Act*. Which song was it?

    a. "Ghost"
    b. "All or None"
    c. "Love Boat Captain"
    d. "You Are"

16. True or False: The band chose the name *Riot Act* because they were sick of trying to come up with a name.

17. True or False: Fans booed Pearl Jam for playing the anti-George W. Bush song "Bu$hleaguer".

18. True or False: The band played a completely different set-list every night on the *Riot Act* tour.

19. During the *Riot Act* tour, the band gave its first press conference in ten years. Where was that press conference held?

    a. Mexico City
    b. Yokohama
    c. St. Louis
    d. Melbourne

20. Which of these acts did NOT open for Pearl Jam on the *Riot Act* tour?

    a. Mudhoney
    b. Buzzcocks
    c. The Melvins

d. Sleater-Kinney

ANSWERS

1. C- Refugees of the Kosovo War: the album was *No Boundaries: A Benefit for The Kosovar Refugees*. Pearl Jam's label Epic released it and included songs from Black Sabbath, Peter Gabriel, and Alanis Morissette. "Last Kiss" led the album off.

2. False: for years, it was claimed that the song was written about the tragic case of Jeanette Clark and J.L. Hancock, who died in an accident at age sixteen in 1962. Apparently, Jeanette's father helped with the bodies' recovery and did not recognize his own daughter. However, it turns out that the song was recorded before these events.

3. A- "If You Had My Love" – Jennifer Lopez: the massive hit was a throw-away single the band intended as a Christmas single for the fan club. Jeff said they had never spent so little on mixing a song and commented, "It was the most minimalist recording we've ever done." Meanwhile, Stone said, "You can try album after album to write a hit and spend months getting drum sounds and rewriting lyrics, or you can go to a used record store and pick out a single and fall in love with it."

4. B- Two microphones, often arranged on the head of a mannequin. The idea is to put the microphones in

a position that creates a 3-D stereo sound sensation for listeners. The mannequin technique is called "dummy head recording," and one microphone is placed in each ear.

5. D- Nebulas: the photos were actual Hubble Space Telescope pictures used with NASA's permission. Jeff explained, "One of the themes that we've been exploring...is just realizing that in the big scheme of things, even the music that we make when we come together, no matter how powerful it is, it's still pretty minuscule. I think for me, the whole space theme has a lot to do with scale. You know, you look at some of those pictures, and there are thirteen light-years in four inches in that picture."

6. True: however, Mike has since turned his life around. He has also focused on helping musicians rehabilitate themselves as he has. In 2018, he received the MusiCares award for his commitment to helping people recover from addiction. Guns N' Roses bassist and fellow Seattle native Duff McKagen gave Mike the award and said, "We've been friends for forty years, I've seen you struggle. I was right there with you. You are always there, always a solid anchor with a smile... Whenever I see you playing guitar, I see the madness and the beauty of an addict being set free."

7. True: the police claimed, "We have spoken to numerous witnesses who have told us that Pearl Jam

are well known for almost appealing for violent behavior." It also blasted "crowd surfing," saying that this had long been practiced at Pearl Jam shows. The band's manager Kelly Curtis responded, "As the band's manager, I find it hard to believe that after all that has transpired, the band's devastation over the [tragedy] that occurred at the Roskilde Festival during their performance, and their long history of attention to fan safety, that anyone would assign 'moral responsibility' to them."

8. False: the Roskilde police released a letter backtracking from all of their accusations.

9. True: Mike said, "I think the thought crossed all of our minds, but it wouldn't have been a good way to end it all. We realized we're making viable music. We can't stop. We can't end on a down note." Instead, the band went on a US tour. Eddie explained that "playing, facing crowds, being together" in the North American tour "enabled us to start processing it."

10. MGM Grand, Las Vegas: they saved the home show at the KeyArena for the last stop of the tour.

11. False: the band never had a problem with fans making their recordings of Pearl Jam shows. They began to issue the Pearl Jam *Official Bootlegs* series so that fans could enjoy a more affordable and better-quality alternative.

12. True: the initial record was set by the first set from their European tours, which had seen five of the show's chart. In the second release, no less than seven of the *Official Bootlegs* charted. They included the shows in Jones Beach, New York; Boston, Massachusetts; Indianapolis, Indiana; Pittsburgh, Pennsylvania; Philadelphia, Pennsylvania; Tampa, Florida; and Memphis, Tennessee.

13. B- "Long Road": the show was featured on all four big networks and organized by George Clooney. Aside from Pearl Jam, it also featured Bruce Springsteen, U2, Stevie Wonder, and Alicia Keys.

14. C- Adam Kasper

15. D- "You Are"

16. True: Vedder said they were just looking for anything decent since they had significant difficulty finding a title. Mike admits that it really doesn't have any significance. He said, "I guess we were trying to come up with a title that reflected some of the music on the record, which we thought was urgent-sounding and kind of loud... It just seemed to fit."

17. True: the band was playing in Long Island. Some of the crowd was chanting "USA! USA!" early in the show. Eddie mocked them, and a very contentious environment emerged. During the song's performance, the singer wore a Bush mask with a

cigar hanging out of his mouth. The show was only about a year and a half after 9/11, and many New Yorkers were not ready for that kind of criticism.

18. True: they always varied their set-list quite a bit and, over the years, have made an effort to change the set-list on every show, especially in the last twenty years.

19. A- Mexico City

20. C- The Melvins

DID YOU KNOW?

- NBA star (and the greatest rebounder to ever play the game) Dennis Rodman credits Pearl Jam for saving his life. He was sitting in his car with a gun outside of the Palace of Auburn Hills. Rodman says listening to Pearl Jam was a "life-changing experience." As he explains, "Something that saved me was the fact that I was listening to Pearl Jam a lot." The former Bulls star Rodman says it was the song "Black" in particular. Rodman became a fan after meeting Eddie Vedder and following the singer's suggestion to check out his band. "I went and got that album [*Ten*], and I would play it every day. For some reason, that song was on; I think that saved my life."

- In 2000, Pearl Jam played at the massive Roskilde Festival in Denmark. The lineup also included Iron Maiden, Oasis, Lou Reed, and many other well-known acts. With that many high-profile acts on the bill, it is no surprise that around 100,000 fans bought tickets to the event. Unfortunately, the large crowd got out of control and crushed nine festival-goers to death. Twenty-six others experienced serious injuries. It appears that the mud on the ground made it difficult for fans to remain on their feet. Eddie remembered, "It was chaos. Some people were yelling, 'thank you.' Others, who weren't in bad shape, were running up and saying 'hi.' Then someone was pulled over, laid out, and they were blue. We knew immediately it had gone on to that other level."

- The great irony of the disaster in Roskilde was that the next song was supposed to be "Alive." Eddie said, "There were still 40,000 people out there," he continued. "They were ready for the show to start again. They started singing, 'I'm still alive.' ...That was when my brain clicked a switch. I knew I would never be the same."

- During the *Binaural* tour, the band began recording every show to release them as live albums. They continue to release their new shows online, with 192K MP3s, a superior format about 50% higher than the standard bit rate. Since they started the series, Pearl Jam has sold over 13 million copies of official bootlegs. The series includes every show the band has played since starting the series, not including all warm-up shows at smaller clubs. All the CD releases were double-disc releases, except the KeyArena show on November 6, 2000, a triple-CD.

- Eddie was almost killed in a boating accident in Hawaii in the early 2000s. He was sailing with some friends, and their boat was overturned. Eddie and two of his friends were stranded and far away from the boat. They were saved by Keith and Ashley Baxter, who happened to be sailing nearby. Vedder was very thankful. In 2013, he brought Ashley onto the stage and dedicated the song "Future Days" to her. A few years later, Keith was in a terrible accident and required a good deal of money for treatment to save his leg. The band contributed $70,000 on GoFundMe to the cause.

CHAPTER 10:

SELF-TITLED ALBUM AND *BACKSPACER*

1. In 2003, the band ended its relationship with Epic Records—the company that had put out all of their albums from *Ten* all the way through to *Riot Act*. Why did the relationship end?

    a. The contract had run its course
    b. Epic fired the band
    c. Pearl Jam left despite a contract
    d. The sides mutually decided to terminate

2. The band's first recording released without a label was a single. Which song was it?

    a. "World Wide Suicide"
    b. "Just Breathe"
    c. "Man of the Hour"
    d. "Love, Reign o'er Me"

3. Who did the band partner with to release the song?

    a. Apple
    b. Amazon

c. Microsoft

d. Google

4. In 2004, Pearl Jam released a live album: *Live at Benaroya Hall*. To release it, they signed a one-album deal with a record company. Which company released it?

    a. Epic
    b. Geffen
    c. BMG
    d. Virgin

5. In 2004, Pearl Jam allowed a TV show to use one of their songs for the first time ever. Which show had that honor?

    a. *Friends*
    b. *House*
    c. *Deadwood*
    d. *Shameless*

6. True or False: The compilation album *Rearviewmirror (Greatest Hits 1991–2003)* had two CDs—one dedicated to the earlier grunge material and the second to their later, more experimental material.

7. Which classic rock radio staple did Pearl Jam cover on their *Live at the Garden* DVD?

    a. "(Don't Fear) The Reaper" – Blue Oyster Cult
    b. "More Than a Feeling" – Boston
    c. "L.A. Woman" – The Doors

d. "Fortunate Son" – Creedence Clearwater Revival

8. In 2005, the band played a benefit show to raise money for Hurricane Katrina at the House of Blues. Where was the show played?

    a. Chicago
    b. Anaheim
    c. Las Vegas
    d. New Orleans

9. Where did the first single of the self-titled *Pearl Jam* album "World Wide Suicide" peak on the *Billboard* Modern Rock Chart?

    a. No. 1
    b. No. 5
    c. No. 10
    d. No. 15

10. How were the songs for the album *Pearl Jam* written?

    a. On the road
    b. Each member wrote them at home
    c. At the recording sessions
    d. A combination of all of the above

11. True or False: Eddie wrote two sets of lyrics for every song on *Pearl Jam*.

12. During the tour supporting the *Pearl Jam* album, the band did a stint opening for another act. Which band was it?

    a. The Rolling Stones
    b. Tom Petty and the Heartbreakers
    c. U2
    d. Radiohead

13. To celebrate their 20th anniversary, the band released a movie called *Pearl Jam Twenty*. Which Hollywood director made it?

    a. Cameron Crowe
    b. Martin Scorsese
    c. Christopher Nolan
    d. Tim Burton

14. True or False: The band located the original *Momma-Son* tapes that Eddie had sent the band when he auditioned for them while working on the *Ten* reissues in 2009.

15. The band finally launched its own record company, releasing its ninth studio album, *Backspacer*. What is the name of the record company?

    a. Third Man Records
    b. Freakout Records
    c. Youth Riot Records
    d. Monkeywrench Records

16. During the tour to support *Backspacer*, Pearl Jam played the final show at what now-defunct arena?

a. Charlotte Colosseum
b. Philadelphia Spectrum
c. The Warehouse
d. John F. Kennedy Stadium

17. In 2011, the band released a live album with a surprisingly studio-sounding feel. What was it called?

a. *Live on Two Legs*
b. *Live on Four Legs*
c. *Live on Ten Legs*
d. *Live on Twenty Legs*

18. Critics noticed that the songs on *Backspacer* had elements of a genre they had never heard before on a Pearl Jam album. What was it?

a. Reggae
b. Progressive Rock
c. Electronic Dance Music
d. New Wave

19. Which Caribbean country did Pearl Jam play for the first time in support of *Backspacer*?

a. Trinidad & Tobago
b. Cuba
c. Costa Rica
d. Jamaica

20. The artwork for *Backspacer* was done by a well-known editorial cartoonist. Who was it?

a. Dan Perkins
b. Walt Handelsman
c. David Horsey
d. Matt Davies

ANSWERS

1. A- The contract had run its course. The band waited patiently for the deal to end and celebrated its newfound freedom once it did. Jeff said, "We're in this amazing position for the first time in twelve years. We can do whatever we want. Even the feeling of being free is exciting."

2. C- "Man of the Hour": the song accompanied the credits of the movie *Big Fish* and appeared on its soundtrack. The band loved the movie. Mike said, "We were so blown away by the movie... Eddie and I were standing around talking about it afterwards and were teary-eyed. We were so emotionally charged and moved by the imagination and humanity that we felt because of the movie."

3. B- Amazon: you could purchase the single either through the official website or Amazon.com.

4. C- BMG: the album is a document of the show held on July 27, 2004, at Benaroya Hall in Seattle. The show had a more acoustic character than most of their shows at that time.

5. A- *Friends:* the song "Yellow Ledbetter" was used in the final episode of the show. It was used as the background for the scene where Rachel prepares to leave Ross for the last time.

6. False: the first side was dedicated to the more straight-ahead rock material. Meanwhile, side two featured slower songs and ballads. The compilation was very well-received and earned four or five stars from just about every media outlet that reviewed it.

7. D- "Fortunate Son" – Creedence Clearwater Revival: the DVD's version was spliced together from several performances and included appearances by Steve Earle, Billy Gibbons, Nancy Wilson, and Johnny Marr.

8. A- Chicago: the $1000 per-ticket event also featured former Led Zeppelin singer Robert Plant and his band The Strange Sensation. You could also get a $25,000 box for the event. The proceeds went to benefit the Red Cross, Habitat for Humanity, the Jazz Foundation of America, and the New Orleans Musicians' Clinic.

9. A- No. 1: it was their first number one on that chart since 1996. The song is an anti-war anthem inspired by former football star Pat Tillman's death in the Afghanistan War. Eddie said, "It's about him and a bunch of the guys who didn't get as much coverage—the guys who barely got a paragraph instead of ten pages...The thing about Tillman was, he got ten pages, but they were all lies. His family is being blocked by our government from finding out what happened...Where are the leaders that are going to represent a galvanized view on what to do

next? ...Democracy might have a chance at working if people educate themselves on these issues and make their opinions known."

10. C- At the recording sessions: for the first time since *Vs.*, the band members showed up with no entirely written songs. They just had a few riffs in mind. Eddie admitted the band "really went in with nothing." This approach led to a very democratic process where each member had some input.

11. False: he wrote at least four sets of lyrics each. In some cases, Eddie would "figure out after eight, nine, or eleven drafts that the first one was the one."

12. B- Tom Petty and the Heartbreakers

13. A- Cameron Crowe: it was a natural fit as Crowe, and the band had worked together on the movie *Singles*. Pearl Jam allowed Crowe to record and gain access to 12,000 hours of footage for the documentary.

14. True: Jeff explained, "I think the first time that Ed or I had opened any of those boxes was a few weeks ago. I knew that the original 'Momma-Son' cassette was somewhere, but I hadn't listened to it in 17, 18, 19 years. It was cool to sit down and play it for the first time with Ed and see his reaction. And to find that 90% of it stayed exactly the same as what ended up on the record. A lot of elements were identical. There was some energy flying

around at that point even from 1,300 miles away from Seattle to San Diego." The reissue was followed by new versions of *Vs.*, *Vitalogy*, *No Code*, and *Yield*.

15. D- Monkeywrench Records was launched in 2014.

16. B- Philadelphia Spectrum

17. C- *Live on Ten Legs*: the album was billed as a sequel to *Live on Two Legs*. The album got positive reviews.

18. D- New Wave: Mike agreed and said, "I'd sum it up as kind of a tight, concise, rock 'n' roll record with kind of pop or maybe new wave elements to it... It's a really quick record, but I like that element to it. I like the sparseness of the songs and the way that Brendan pulled us together and made us play as good as we could."

19. C- Costa Rica: before 30,000 ecstatic fans. Eddie greeted them in Spanish, saying, "Hello, Costa Rica, our band is twenty years old, but we're still young. I don't know why we've never come to Costa Rica, but we're very happy to be here. We left the best for last."

20. A- Dan Perkins: he was working for *Village Voice Media* when many of their outlets went under. Eddie commissioned him in support, and Dan spent six months on the gorgeous artwork of the album.

DID YOU KNOW?

- In 2003, Pearl Jam released *Lost Dogs* through their former record company Epic, which owned the songs. It is a compilation of B-sides and unreleased songs. The album includes a hidden track tribute to deceased Alice in Chains singer Layne Staley. There were some controversial omissions from the album, most notably the two (excellent) songs from the Merkin Ball E.P.: "I Got Id" and "Long Road". It also proved that an album of discarded cuts from Pearl Jam is better than most other bands' top material. As the review on *AllMusic* states, "*Lost Dogs* crackles with that passion, and it has another advantage: unlike most of Pearl Jam's albums, it's a fun, compulsive listen. More than any other album in its catalog, *Lost Dogs* captures what Pearl Jam stood for and what it felt like at their peak."

- After leaving Epic to gain some freedom, Pearl Jam found themselves back under the same company's roof within a few years. In the interim between *Riot Act* and the recording of *Pearl Jam*, the band had been distracted and had not prepared their platform for music releases. Therefore, they signed a one-album deal with J Records, which Clive Davis ran at the time. Eddie said that they believed J Records was "somebody who'll allow us to be who we are and respect how we do things" while still "getting the music out there." Funnily enough, J Records was purchased soon after by Sony. Sony, of course, is the same company that owns Epic Records. Therefore, Pearl Jam found themselves under the same ownership.

- *Pearl Jam* was the most political album the band had ever recorded. The band was frustrated that George W. Bush had been reelected. Also, Eddie noted that the birth of his daughter Olivia had focused him on more topical issues: "Now that I see it as my daughter's planet, I'm even more (angry)." Therefore, several songs focus on the Iraq War, while others engage with issues such as poverty and religion in public life.

- The band began a planned reissue of their entire back catalog in 2009. They released four different versions of the classic debut album *Ten* that year. They included a Brendan O'Brien remix of the album, which was a bit rawer than the original and had less reverb. Jeff Ament reprised his role as a designer, which he had played on the original, and came up with the packaging alongside Andy Fischer of Cameron Crowe's Vinyl Films. Jeff explained, "The original concept was about really being together as a group and entering into the world of music as a true band... a sort of all-for-one deal. There were some elements of the original *Ten* artwork that didn't turn out the way we had hoped due to time constraints. With this reissue, we've been able to take our time and invest resources into making the design the way we had originally intended."

- *Backspacer* saw Pearl Jam turning back the clock in more ways than one. They renewed their partnership with Brendan O'Brien and debuted at No. 1 for the first time since *Yield*. It was also the most optimistic album the band had recorded in years. The band attributes that to the election of *Barack* Obama in 2008.

CHAPTER 11:

LIGHTNING BOLT AND GIGATON

1. True or False: The band's tenth album, *Lightning Bolt*, was considered Pearl Jam's return to form album.

2. True or False: *Lightning Bolt* debuted at No. 2 on the *Billboard* album charts.

3. The band recorded seven tracks at Henson Recording Studio in L.A. They then took a break from recording. When they returned, what did they think of the tracks they had laid down at Henson?

   a. It was the best material they had ever recorded
   b. It was garbage
   c. It wasn't good enough to be the basis of the album
   d. Very little work remained to be done

4. Which of the songs on *Lightning Bolt* had previously appeared on Eddie's solo album *Ukulele Songs*?

a. "Pendulum"
b. "Mind Your Manners"
c. "Sleeping by Myself"
d. "Yellow Moon"

5. On the rocking single "Mind Your Manners," Mike said he was trying to emulate which band?

a. Dead Kennedys
b. Black Flag
c. The Stooges
d. The Damned

6. Which show on the *Lightning Bolt* tour was interrupted, ironically enough, by the fear of a lightning bolt hitting?

a. London, Ontario
b. Chicago, Illinois
c. Amsterdam, Netherlands
d. Cincinnati, Ohio

7. In 2015, Pearl Jam won a Grammy for Best Packaging. How many Grammys had they won previously?

a. None
b. One
c. Four
d. Seven

8. When Pearl was nominated for Best Packaging in 2015, it was not the first time they had been

nominated for the award. How many nominations had they received, including that one?

    a. Five nominations

    b. Ten nominations

    c. Fifteen nominations

    d. Twenty nominations

9. Which of these Pearl Jam drummers was inducted into the Hall of Fame with the band?

    a. Dave Abbruzzese

    b. Jack Irons

    c. Matt Chamberlain

    d. Dave Krusen

10. True or False: The band invited the drummers who were not inducted into the Hall of Fame to the ceremony.

11. True or False: In 2018, Pearl Jam released the single "Can't Deny Me," announcing it would be on the upcoming *Gigaton* album. However, despite reaching No. 11 on the Mainstream Rock charts, it was left off the album.

12. True or False: *Gigaton* is Pearl Jam's shortest album.

13. Which classic rock band is referenced by name in the song "Quick Escape?"

    a. Queen

    b. Led Zeppelin

    c. The Who

d. The Doors

14. Which song on *Gigaton* was written by all the members of the band?

    a. "Seven O'Clock"
    b. "Dance of the Clairvoyants"
    c. "Never Destination"
    d. "Retrograde"

15. In which country did "Dance of the Clairvoyants" reach No. 1 in the charts?

    a. Poland
    b. New Zealand
    c. Belgium
    d. Croatia

16. True or False: *Gigaton* debuted at No. 1 in the *Billboard* album charts.

17. In what year did the band finally release their iconic *Unplugged* set on vinyl and CD?

    a. 2017
    b. 2018
    c. 2019
    d. 2020

18. True or False: Eddie finished working on the soundtrack to Sean Penn's film *Flag Day* just before COVID-19 forced the US economy's shutdown.

19. When did Eddie join Instagram?

    a. He hasn't

b. In 2018

c. In 2019

d. In 2020

20. Who produced *Gigaton*?

    a. Josh Evans

    b. Brendan O'Brien

    c. Butch Vig

    d. Jeff Ament

ANSWERS

1. True: for example, *The Guardian* called it "a sturdy return to great form." But also, a trick question. It seems like every album Pearl Jam has released since *Yield* has been considered a 'comeback' album of some kind. But the truth is, there was nothing to come back from. Pearl Jam has consistently put out great albums for thirty years now.

2. False: the album debuted at No. 1 (where it belonged). It joined the other Pearl Jam albums to do so: *Vs.*, *Vitalogy*, *No Code*, and *Backspacer*.

3. C- It wasn't good enough to be the basis of the album. Therefore, the band regrouped for six weeks of intense recording sessions to finish the album.

4. C- "Sleeping by Myself": Brendan O'Brien encouraged the band to reinterpret the song since it was "a Pearl Jam song as far as I'm concerned."

5. A- Dead Kennedys

6. B- Chicago, Illinois: the show was delayed for a good two hours. However, the Chicago Police Department allowed the band to continue playing past the normal curfew. The warning was not without good reason, as some powerful lightning bolts hit right near the stadium while the fans

waited. The band had a treat for Chicago Cubs fans when they brought on legendary Hall of Fame shortstop Ernie Banks to sing a chorus of the team song "All the Way." Eddie is a lifelong Cubs fan and said, "I think growing up being a fan of the Chicago Cubs, it was an intense and truly remarkable character builder. Anything that you had to face adversity and that you had to face setbacks, having been a fan of the Chicago Cubs allowed you to stay strong and persevere and never lose hope and have faith that someday your team would go all the way."

7. B- One: the band had won the Grammy for Best Hard Rock Performance in 1996 for the song "Spin the Black Circle." Eddie said in his acceptance speech, "I don't know what this means," he said. "I don't think it means anything. That's just how I feel. There's too many bands, and you've heard it all before. My dad would've liked it; my dad died before I got to know him. He would've liked it, so that's why I'm here. Thanks, I guess."

8. C- Fifteen: yup, what is most aggravating is that *Vs.*, *Vitalogy*, and *Backspacer* were nominated for Best Rock Album and lost each time. To whom? To the Rolling Stones in 1995, Alanis Morrissette in 1996, and Muse in 2011. *Ten* was not nominated at all, but "Jeremy" was for two awards.

9. D- Dave Krusen: it was pretty amazing to think that Jack Irons and Dave Abbruzzese were not inducted despite providing some of the best drumming work of the 1990s. Dave was not very happy about it. "So... Rock & Roll Hall of Fucktardia. Ergh," he wrote on Facebook. "It makes absolutely zero sense to me... I'm just gonna shove this statement up someone's arse." Fans put together a petition calling for his inclusion.

10. True: or maybe false! After being snubbed by the committee, Dave Abbruzzese challenged the current members of Pearl Jam to invite him. He said, "They can't justify ignoring my contributions. Like me or not. If there is still a part of that band that remembers how hard we worked, how much blood, and how much sweat... They will do the right thing." The band released a measured statement, noting that awards are "subjective" and saying that the band looked forward to reuniting with "Dave Krusen, Matt Chamberlin, Dave Abbruzzese, and Jack Irons, who are each individually great players who gave their all to the early recordings and live gigs. Looking forward to seeing them and all the other musicians on the bill." However, Dave says the band never contacted him.

11. True

12. False. It is actually the longest album they ever released. At fifty-seven minutes, it's two minutes

longer than *Vitalogy*, which was the second-longest. Meanwhile, at just thirty-seven minutes, *Backspacer* was the shortest.

13. A- Queen. The line is "Queen cranking on the blaster / and Mercury did rise." However, if you said Led Zeppelin, you are not entirely wrong. The song does reference their classic Kashmir as well.

14. B- "Dance of the Clairvoyants": the band was particularly excited about this song. Jeff said, "'Dance' was a perfect storm of experimentation and real collaboration, mixing up the instrumentation and building a great song, and Ed writing some of my favorite words yet, around Matt's killer drum pattern. Did I mention Mike's insane guitar part and that Stone is playing bass on this one? We've opened some new doors creatively, and that's exciting."

15. A- Poland

16. False: not this time. *Gigaton* debuted at No. 5.

17. 17 D- 2020: the album was released to mark the 30th anniversary of the band's existence.

18. False: Eddie and his collaborators Glen Hansard and Cat Power had to figure out how to complete it during the lockdown.

19. D- In 2020: he did so in the hope of influencing the 2020 General Elections. Eddie said, "Disseminating

some positive information. I will try to keep it interesting and maybe artistic. [But] I realized there was something I agreed wholeheartedly with Donald Trump in regards to [this being] no doubt the most important election in our country's history. Finally, we agreed on something. Let's make sure we can vote by mail in places where we can."

20. A- Josh Evans

DID YOU KNOW?

- The recording *Lightning Bolt* was delayed because the members of the band were focused on side projects. Eddie had launched a successful solo tour to back his solo album *Ukulele Songs*. Meanwhile, Stone had reunited his long-time band, Brad. Jeff released a solo album named *While My Heart Beats*. Mike was part of a reunion of Mad Season. Finally, Matt Cameron was part of a Soundgarden reunion album and tour. It was without a doubt the most attention the band as a whole had spent on side projects. Eddie said that paradoxically, the period away had resulted in "more importance placed on the records" and focusing on making the best album possible.

- The central theme of the lyrics on *Lightning Bolt* is mortality. As Stone explained, "[At] 40-something, almost 50-something, you're looking at life through your kids' eyes, through the filter of relationships that are twenty or thirty-years-long, through the filter of your parents getting older and the passing of friends and relatives—relationships and all that they encompass, the difficulties of them and the sacrifices you make in them and also the joy they bring you." Eddie was hesitant to talk about mortality, but relented and focused on the theme, realizing it could help him and others cope and offer help in "getting through it." The song "Future Days" was difficult for Eddie to write as it was on his friend Dennis Flemion, who drowned a few years previously.

- When the band was rightfully inducted into the Hall of Fame in 2017, Neil Young was slated to introduce them at the ceremony, which took place at the Barclays Center in Brooklyn. However, his health was bad. Instead, David Letterman was brought in at the last minute to give the induction speech. Eddie's speech was typical, starting with an acknowledgment of "all those who came before us," naming the "tetrapods, the primates, the homo erectus" before warning of the dangers of climate change. The band played "Alive," "Given to Fly," and "Better Man."

- *Gigaton* has a solid environmental concept. The cover shows melting icecaps. Scientists use the term "gigaton" to measure the pace at which ice is melting in the poles. This pace has been increasing substantially in recent years. The band also invited climate change activist Greta Thunberg to feature in the song "Retrograde's" music video. In the video, the impressive seventeen-year old explains what the planet's future will look like if significant changes are not made regarding sustainability and our environmental footprint.

- In May 2017, Chris Cornell committed suicide by hanging. Eddie was hit hard by his death and told Howard Stern, "I've had to be somewhat in denial. I don't even feel like I had a choice. I was just terrified where I would go if I allowed myself to feel what I needed to feel or what I instinctively wanted to feel, or how dark I felt like I was gonna go." Kurt Cobain had died in 1994. Layne Staley in 2002. These tragedies left Eddie as the last of the singers of the big Seattle bands still standing. Amongst their contemporaries, the band has proven an oasis of stability and longevity.

CONCLUSION

We hope you enjoyed this exploration of the career of Pearl Jam. Starting from their roots in Green River and Mother Love Bone and through to their latest releases, this Seattle band has always been faithful to their roots and vision. Rather than follow trends or prove points to critics and trendsetters, they have made their music and created a passionate and long-lasting following of hardcore fans. Considering how good their last album *Gigtaon* is (latest at the time of writing, that is), we know that there are great things ahead from this magnificent band.

Made in the USA
Las Vegas, NV
30 October 2022

58394200R00079